Olivier

Olivier

Francis Beckett

HAUS PUBLISHING • LONDON

First published in Great Britain in 2005 by
Haus Publishing Limited
26 Cadogan Court
London SW3 3BX

Copyright © Francis Beckett, 2005

The moral right of the author has been asserted

A CIP catalogue record for this book
is available from the British Library

ISBN 1-904950-38-8 (paperback)

Designed and typeset in Garamond
Printed and bound by Graphicom in Vicenza, Italy

Front cover: photograph of Laurence Olivier courtesy of Album akg Images

Contents

The outer fringes of gentility

It's no accident that the generation born just after the turn of the century produced the greatest array of theatrical talent for many generations. Ralph Richardson was born in 1903, John Gielgud in 1904, Michael Redgrave in 1908; and 1907 saw the birth of perhaps the greatest and certainly the most influential actor Britain has ever seen, Laurence Olivier. Theirs was a lucky generation, too young to have their lives destroyed by the First World War and too old to have their youth blighted by the Second.

Men born half a decade or so earlier were sent to fight, often to die and generally to lose most of their male friends and be permanently scarred, mentally and physically, in the four-year earthquake we know as the First World War, but which, in the twenties and thirties, they called simply the Great War. However much they rebelled, they were still Edwardians. A part of them still harked back to the world before the war, still hankered after the happiness and moral certainty they thought had filled it. Men born half a decade or so later had their consciousness scarred, and their lives circumscribed, by the vicious sectarian politics of the thirties and the brutal realities of the dictatorships run by Hitler, Mussolini and Stalin; and they ended up giving their young manhood to the fight against Hitler.

The twenties was a liberated decade, artistically and sexually – at least by comparison with the previous 100 years and the next 30 years. In the 1930s Britain started to button up again, and did not begin another round of unbuttoning until the 1960s. Olivier's generation enjoyed the new freedoms and optimism of the 1920s, and flourished in the revival of a newly invigorated theatre. They did not mourn a pre-war world they had hardly known. By the time the Second World War arrived, they were eminent enough to be able to make a greater contribution to the war effort by their art than they could make by stopping a bullet.

The golden boy of this golden generation was Laurence Kerr Olivier, born on 22 May 1907 at 26 Wathen Road, Dorking, Surrey. His memoirs do not even mention the Great War, though it began when he was seven and ended when he was 11. His father, Gerard Kerr Olivier, was an Anglican priest and former schoolmaster, who in 1907 was ministering to a small flock in Dorking. Gerard Olivier's loud, resonant voice and histrionic pulpit manner made his sermons famous. He was certain and rigid in his opinions, and liked to be the master in his own house. A follower of the Oxford Movement, he was the sort of High Church priest who likes to adopt Roman Catholic ritual, and to call himself Father like a Catholic priest. It is, of course, the most theatrical of all Christian traditions, enabling Father Olivier – and in due course his son Laurence – to strut majestically in sweeping robes and wave caskets of incense, filling the air with sweet, mystical scents.

When Laurence, the youngest of his three children, was three, Gerard Olivier took his family to live in Notting Hill, West London, while he earned a precarious living as a kind of supply priest, filling in while the local priest was on holiday. After two years of this he found a new parish in Pimlico, south London, and the family moved to 22 Lupus Street.

The sound of Gerard Olivier's name reflected his French Huguenot ancestry, as did the names he gave his children: Sybille, born in 1901; Gerard Dacres, born in 1904 and known in the family as Dickie; and the baby of the family, Laurence (rather than the anglicised Lawrence). It was a devout and moderately distinguished family and Gerard Olivier boasted several clergymen among his ancestors. They always insisted on pronouncing Olivier in the French manner.

Olivier's cousin, the distinguished genealogist Jeremy Gibson, tells me that the first known Olivier was Laurent Olivier, born around 1520 in Nay, France, and it is likely that Gerard knew of him and named his son after him. The family was still at Nay when his great-great-grandson Jourdain Olivier studied for the church, and as a Huguenot was attacked by the Jesuits, imprisoned, and banished from France in 1685. He became a protégé of William of Orange at The Hague where he was a minister, and is thought to have come to England with William when William became king of England.

The family prospered in England. One of Jourdain's grandsons was a wealthy banker. Another descendent made a fortune as a diamond merchant. And they tended only to have one son every generation, which kept the money in the family. Laurence's great grandfather Henry Olivier was a colonel in the army and high sherriff of Wiltshire in 1843.

There was money in the family. Yet Gerard seems to have been obsessed with his own poverty, in the special way of fading Edwardian gentlefolk. He was the youngest son of a youngest son, and his own father had been a parson too; what was once an ample fortune had been spread wide and thin, and the parson, with little by way of inheritance, seems to have been haunted by the spectre of poverty lurking beneath his veneer of gentility.

He was always intended for the ministry, but at first he became a teacher instead, finding a job in a Guildford preparatory school and meeting and marrying the headmaster's sister-in-law. But he later rediscovered his vocation and was ordained in the Church of England in 1903. He kept up appearances, kept servants, sent his children to public schools (though cheap ones which gave clergy a discount) and found endless ways of saving pennies.

His older brothers were substantially richer. One of them, Sydney Haldane Olivier, was a top civil servant and an eminent Fabian socialist with a distinguished career in the Colonial Office, becoming Sir Sydney in 1907 and Governor of Jamaica from 1907 to 1913.

Sydney was a civil servant during the First World War, retiring in 1920 – but still, as we shall see, with an important political role to fulfil. He once stayed with Gerard's family, and Laurence's father splashed out on vintage port and good food. In later years Laurence Olivier based his Shylock on Uncle Sydney, who according to Bernard Shaw looked like a Spanish grandee.

Laurence Olivier always remembered how his father had perfected the art of carving a joint so thinly that he could cover a respectable portion of the plate with a tiny portion of meat, and then say: 'There, get that outside you and you won't do badly.' He encouraged his children to be sparing in the use of toilet paper, and allotted a small quantity of water in which he and his sons would take turns to bathe, so Laurence remembered always washing in dirty, tepid bathwater.

Though Olivier became far richer than his father could ever have dreamed of being, the parsimony in his father which he mocks mercilessly was a characteristic he seems to have inherited. His memoirs are full of sideways glances at the unacceptably high cost of things. He is said to have always secretly turned down the thermostat on his heated swim-

Laurence Olivier's father perfected the art of carving a joint so thinly that he could cover a respectable portion of the plate with a tiny portion of meat.

ming pool, and when, late in life, he had a son in his third marriage, he resented being forced to pay the high fees demanded by a public school. He seems to have been affronted at the idea that, by paying these fees out of taxed income, he was subsidising the state education of children from much poorer families.

Laurence Olivier was not close to his father. Perhaps it was the Reverend's parsimony, perhaps his grandson Tarquin Olivier is right and Gerard was incapable of love, or perhaps it was simply that fathers in middle class Edwardian families thought it proper to keep some distance between them and their children. Whatever the reason, all of young Laurence's love went to his mother Agnes, born Agnes Crookenden, from a family of teachers. It was a love that lasted all his life, and affected his relationship with every woman he became close to, including the three women he married. Adults who knew her remember her as dark, lively, competent. Her daughter Sybille once said: 'She was the most enchanting person. Hair so long she could sit on it. She absolutely made our childhood. Always saw the funny side of everything. She adored Larry. He was hers.'

Her beloved Larry remembered her in his seventies like this: *My mother was lovely – there is no photograph that I have ever seen that has revealed this in anything like its true measure.* She returned his love in full measure: he was always the favourite of her three children.

Even the fact that, between the ages of five and nine, she used regularly to beat him with a hairbrush on his naked bottom for telling lies was turned into an example of her saintly nature. Probably, he mused, she did it because otherwise his father would beat him much more severely (in most Edwardian families, the father would administer beatings when they were deemed necessary). *How much the nobler then, my mother's voluntary self-punishment* he writes without a hint of irony. He was sure that it really did hurt her more than it hurt him. She told him so herself: 'How I wish you wouldn't persist in making this hateful business necessary.' On one of these painful occasions young Laurence *noticed . . . while I was removing the necessary garments that she was in a state of high distress.* The two strokes she once excused him – the tariff was six strokes but she stopped at four because he was being brave about it – meant more to him than the dozens of strokes she did administer.

Her death was the greatest tragedy of his life. There is a sense in which he never recovered. *My heaven, my hope, my entire world, my own worshipped Mummy died when I was 12* he wrote. It must have been made even worse by the pain in which she died. She suffered from glioblastoma, a malignant tumour of the central nervous system. There was a progressive and rapid loss of function, constant pressure in her cranium causing dreadful headaches, constant vomiting. Her last words to Laurence were: 'Darling Larry, no matter what your father says, be an actor. Be a great actor. For me.'

In her last days she begged her husband, after she was gone, to be kind to the baby of the family, and also to send him to Rugby, one of Britain's top public schools. But Laurence had it fixed in his mind, from his earliest years and throughout his life, that his father *couldn't see the slightest purpose in my existence.* He already had a son and a daughter, so *I was an entirely unnecessary extra burden on the exchequer; he would describe how the enormous amount of porridge that I consumed at breakfast put him in a bad temper for the whole day.* After his mother's death, the little boy's need for friendship and love was satisfied, not by his father – who does not seem to have been a cruel man, but was clearly unable to express love – but by his brother and sister.

Nonetheless, Gerard Olivier promised his dying wife to try as hard as he could, and he probably did his stiff and clumsy best. Rugby, however, was out of the question, even though his wife had tried to leave enough money in her will from her own family's fortune, and even though Gerard himself had been educated at the even more splendid Winchester. Laurence's brother Dickie had gone to a much less prestigious school, Radley, but even Radley's comparatively modest fees were out of reach for Gerard's second son. There were, however, a few much less grand places which offered cut-rate places for the sons of clergy. Parsons, it was accepted, needed special treatment, for most of them were like Gerard Olivier: the youngest of a huge Victorian family, sent into the church when their older brothers had occupied better paid professions, with the smallest share of the family fortune and the lowest paid occupation.

One such school was St Edwards in Oxford, and that, after a succession of different preparatory schools, was where Laurence Olivier was dispatched in 1920 at the age of 13, a year after his mother's death. By then the family had moved to Letchworth, and the family fortunes were slightly improved when Gerard sold the rectory and moved to a cheaper modern house.

Laurence was miserable at St Edwards. The less well known public schools founded as recently as the nineteenth century were often even harsher and more spartan than the likes of Eton and Rugby, hoping perhaps to make up in brutality what they lacked in antiquity. Olivier, who shone in the choir and as an actor, was, he says, known to all the other boys as 'that sidey little shit Olivier.'

A young Laurence Olivier, 1915

He was no good at games. And he had what was, in that sort of school, always the most dreadful misfortune: he was a pretty little boy.

He already knew the trouble this inevitably brought in English private schools, for he had been to several preparatory schools, culminating in All Saints Choir School in Marylebone, London, where a bigger and older boy had once thrown him down on the floor and started to rape him before being frightened off by a noise. A prep school master with a specially fashioned strap for beating boys had singled him out for frequent sadistic punishment. *With my trousers down I was made to bend over – 'Bend more tight, bend more tight' he always said; angled to his satisfaction, he laid it onto my bare flesh until my screams reached the vicarage across the courtyard.* The man was eventually fired, mainly because Laurence's brother Dickie was head boy at that school and took the matter up with the headmaster.

But St Edwards was worse than anything he had seen at prep schools. He went there, no doubt, still unconsciously grieving for the mother he had lost the previous year. The prefects caned with a vigour that no prep school master could ever muster. They caned Laurence a lot because he rewarded them by screaming louder than most boys, and because he was a pretty boy. When he was to be caned, other boys gathered in the quad outside the sixth form room to listen to his desperate shrieks. There was not much fun to be had at boarding schools, and listening to Olivier screaming in pain and terror was as good as it got. They called him 'a flirt' but he told friends later in life that it went far further than that: he willingly submitted to the sexual advances of older boys. Of course, this was the small change of life in a British upper class boarding school right up to the 1950s.

Of course, all the characteristics that made Olivier unpopular and eminently beatable in the dirty, repressed, violent atmosphere of traditional English private education for boys were those of a born actor. Even the lies for which his mother beat him were not, as far as it is possible to tell, the normal lies told by a small boy who hopes to get away with a misdeed or manipulate his parents into giving him a treat. They were imaginative, motiveless lies, and told with such assurance and aplomb that at first they were believed. They were the first unconscious stage exercises of a boy who was born to be an actor.

Another was an improvised stage in the nursery of the Pimlico house: a wooden chest, placed against the window, with the curtains arranged round it and candles for footlights, from which the five-year-old boy declaimed passages from plays to an appreciative audience of his mother and sister. A third was his performance in the choir at All Saints Choir School Church, a High Anglican choir school with a splendid musical reputation, which his mother was determined he should enter, but which turned him down several times before finally accepting him and, seeing his talent, made him the soloist. The choir also performed the first half of Shakespeare's *Julius Caesar*, and nine-year-old Olivier was given the part of Brutus. The legendary actress Ellen Terry saw the production and wrote in her diary: 'The small boy who played Brutus is already a great actor.' Soon after, Olivier told the play's director, Father Geoffrey Heald, that he wanted to be an actor.

The next year they performed some scenes from *Twelfth Night*, and Olivier had the plum female part of Maria. With a boy playing Maria, they decided to have a girl playing Sir Toby Belch, and the part was taken by a churchwarden's daughter called Ethel McGlinchey, who changed her name to Fabia Drake and became a highly thought-of Shakespearean actress. And the next year he was Katherina in *The Taming of the Shrew*.

Just before leaving to go to St Edwards, Olivier sang his last solo – and it was his first failure, the first experience of that stage fright which was to come back in old age to haunt him. *My voice faltered, the breath left my being and could not be retrieved, my throat closed up and I was forced to stop.*

Of course the skills he learned from the choirmaster – the Revd Geoffrey Heald, his first theatrical mentor, to whom he remained grateful all his life – were nothing but a burden to him

Olivier in school production of *The Taming of the Shrew*

at St Edwards. He must have had a slightly affected manner, and, it seems, his experience of playing women's parts and making himself feel right in them gave him a manner which seemed to other boys to be effeminate. To add to his trouble, the school ordered him to join the choir, and made him the soloist. No wonder he felt shunned by his peers.

He even tried to avoid being cast in plays, so as to lessen his visibility and the impression that he was different from the others. But in schools like that, whatever is not compulsory is forbidden, and whatever is not forbidden is compulsory; and when the call came, at Christmas 1923 when he was 16, he had no choice but to play Puck. He put his heart and his talent into it, and much to his surprise, his success made him, not more unpopular, but less so.

Until that time, rather surprisingly, Laurence Olivier does not seem to have made any effort to become an actor, despite his beloved mother's last words to him. Perhaps he thought his father would veto the idea, and he seems still to have been frightened of his father. Acting was not considered a reputable profession, nor a job for a gentleman. But very shortly after his triumph as Puck, when he went home for the holidays, his father suddenly proved that he was not quite the remote, uncaring figure Laurence had always supposed.

The two of them were alone in the bathroom, taking turns with the bathwater. They had that morning taken Laurence's brother Dickie to Waterloo: he was off to be a rubber planter in India, and was likely to be away for as much as nine years, during which they would not see him. His father might never see his older son again.

This is Olivier's own account of what happened: *Lowering myself into the water which was, I noticed unhappily, a little cleaner than usual, I snatched the hot tap on for the allotted number of seconds, and after a minute or so I asked my father how soon I might reckon on being allowed to follow Dickie to India. My father's answer was so astonishing that it gave me quite a deep shock: 'Don't be such a fool, you're not going to India, you're going on the stage. 'Am I?' I stammered lamely.*

Gerard Olivier knew his late wife had been right: he had a fine actor for a son. He planned for his son to go to the Central School of Speech Training and Dramatic Art, where his sister Sybille had learned to act, that very summer. But it was not easy: he need hardly have reminded his son that he was not a rich man. So young Laurence was to tell Miss Elsie Fogerty, who ran the school, that he had to insist of being given both a scholarship and a £50 bursary, otherwise there was no chance of him attending since his father could not pay. 'You will of course achieve a scholarship – she will see at once that you are a born actor' added Gerard Olivier.

He was right. Elsie Fogerty heard Laurence's audition piece (the seven ages of man speech from *As You Like It* – 'All the

Peggy Ashcroft at the start of her brilliant career

world's a stage/ And all the men and women merely players . . .') and offered him a scholarship at once. He asked anxiously if he might have the bursary too, and she said she might discuss that in a while. He pressed the point: his father had told him he could not afford to come without the bursary. She looked at him. 'That seems to mean that without our bursary you cannot become an actor' she said, and he nodded miserably. So she gave him the bursary too.

So in the summer of 1924 Larry Olivier, as his friends called him for the rest of his life, left forever the painful confines of St Edwards and moved to London, where he lived on his own, poor but free, and spent his days learning the only skill that seemed to matter to him.

It must have been a wonderful moment of fulfilment and liberation, but £50 was a pretty meagre sum to see him through the year, and his father declined to help. Most of his fellow students were both far richer and far more versed in the ways of the world and the theatre, for the 17-year-old Olivier had mainly known grim clergymen, even grimmer schoolmasters, and sadistic schoolmates. But as an acting pupil, he shone at once, and managed to get vacation jobs at Christmas and Easter in a small theatre in Letchworth, as assistant stage manager, understudy, and sometimes actor, for £4 a week. The Central School's teaching was done in the Royal Albert Hall, and at the end of his year there, Olivier played Shylock in *The Merchant of Venice* and shared considerable plaudits with his Portia, Peggy Ashcroft. The world was soon to hear a great deal of both of them.

From Thorndike to Coward

In 1924, when Olivier went to the Central School, his uncle Sydney Olivier's career had a kind of Indian summer, in every respect: in his retirement he was appointed Secretary of State for India in the 1924 Labour government. He was also created Baron Olivier of Ramsden, the first Lord Olivier (Laurence eventually becoming the second). Labour's first Prime Minister, Ramsay MacDonald, had a low opinion of the Labour politicians who surrounded him, and was pleased with the chance of appointing a career civil servant who was also a member of the Fabian Society. Sydney Olivier had an understanding of race issues that was decades ahead of his time, rejecting what he called 'the shortsighted theory that the dividing habits of race are permanently stronger than the unifying power of humanity.'

The government fell, and Sydney Olivier returned to his retirement and his books. But the twenties – as liberating a decade in their time as the sixties was to be – was a fiercely exciting time for a young man to be footloose and fancy free, albeit penniless, in London, and Laurence Olivier rejoiced in the occasional company of bright young things, from one of whom he learned to dance the newest dance craze, the Charleston; and from American films, almost the only films available in the twenties, he learned the liberating swashbuckling and sexual magnetism of such figures as Douglas Fairbanks Senior and Ronald Colman (early in his acting career he affected a Ronald Colman moustache).

That same year Laurence's father Gerard remarried and became rector of Addington, a small Berkshire parish; his new wife Isobel instantly endeared herself to her three grown-up step-children. And Laurence himself began the dispiriting business known to every young actor in every generation: looking for work. This tests whether you really want to be an actor. Olivier must have wanted it very much. He no longer had Elsie Fogerty's £50 bursary, nor any money at all from his father. The priority for the few pennies he had went on advertising his services in the weekly theatre page of the *Daily Telegraph*: 'Laurence Olivier at liberty.' Food came a poor second to the *Daily Telegraph*.

He still followed his father's religion, and every Sunday found him at All Saints Church, in whose choir he had sung as a small boy. One day the vicar, noticing how undernourished he looked, wrote to his father suggesting an allowance of £1 a week for a few weeks. It made all the difference – Olivier had been eating half a sandwich for supper for a week.

His religion may have found a way of getting him food, but it deprived him of something else his body was demanding with equal urgency – sex. He took entirely seriously, just as seriously as his priestly father, the church's view that sex before marriage was a mortal sin. He has claimed, and there is no reason to disbelieve him, that he had no 'romantic adventures' before his marriage. This abstinence did, however, weigh heavily upon the young actor, a weight only partly eased by what he calls, with typical elaborate evasion, an uneasy compromise with his conscience. He probably means masturbation, though it may be that he visited prostitutes.

His first proper part was in a 'curtain-raiser' – a short play performed before the main play of the evening. Curtain-raisers were common before the First World War, but were starting to fall into disuse by the 1920s. This one was called *The Unfailing Instinct*, by Julian Frank. It seems to have been a pretty wretched play. Olivier describes it with that contempt which actors show for a bad playwright:

(Ruby Miller) was 'Zee Grande Fraunsh actrice' who had been prevailed on by an old lover to give a gracious interview to a young boy – me – still in his teens, who had developed an adoring craze for her. Within a giddily short space of time she had divined that I was none other than her own son. I don't think I'll go on, I might spoil it.

Though intended as a curtain-raiser, its first performance was part of a variety evening at the Brighton Hippodrome. Other acts were famous singers and comedians, including the great Harry Lauder, the most popular standup comic of his day and the darling of the music halls. Olivier was warned several times that the Hippodrome was an old-fashioned theatre with a sill at the side of the stage, which unwary actors had been known to trip over. But he forgot, and the first entrance of his professional career was also one of the most dramatic: he fell headlong, his face coming to rest in the footlights. There was a torrent of laughter from the packed house, and when he eventually left the stage, they gave him a round of applause.

The next day *The Unfailing Instinct* took its rightful place as a curtain-raiser in Manchester. The main event was a full-length play by the same author, called *The Ghost Train.* The two plays did the rounds of provincial theatres for a while – Olivier was an understudy in *The Ghost Train* – in the then traditional try-out run, during which the management could decide whether a production was likely to succeed in the West End. It did not go into the West End, and at the end of the tryout run Olivier was again unemployed. (Later *The Ghost Train* enjoyed a successful West End run.) After weeks of trying he got another job with the Lena Ashwell Players.

Lena Ashwell was by then in her fifties and had become, as many of the most distinguished actors became, an actor-manager, running her own company and starring in its plays. George Bernard Shaw once describing her as 'the divinely-gifted Lena Ashwell'. During the war she had organised companies of actors to entertain the soldiers. By the time the Armistice was signed she had 25 such companies which had played to the troops in France, Malta, Egypt and Palestine, as well as various military camps in England and in London hospitals, and she was awarded the OBE for her services to the war effort.

Working, as she had done in the war, in unusual venues with minimal scenery and props, appealed to her – partly for the remarkably modern reason that it was a way of bringing theatre to audiences which might otherwise never have access to it. The Lena Ashwell Players worked in village halls and similar small venues. Hers was one of the few companies which brought theatre to the smaller communities of the London suburbs; but her plays also had three weeks at her own London theatre in Notting Hill.

It was not to the ambitious young Olivier's taste at all. The wages she paid were low, and he was snobbishly irritated at being expected to perform one night stands in *unthought parts of London* like Deptford, Islington, Shadwell, Shoreditch, Limehouse, *and a few others that the memory boggles at.* He disliked playing in town halls and boarded-over swimming pools where the cast sometimes had to change in the lavatories – Olivier called them 'the lavatory players.' A young actor with no other work does not walk out on a job, but it looks as though he was courting dismissal. He took to silly tricks to amuse the company, like pulling the drapes so that another actor on the stage suddenly caught sight of near-naked female cast members who were changing behind it, which, with any luck, caused the actor to 'corpse', or laugh uncontrollably and out of character.

It couldn't last. It ended while he was playing played Flavius in Shakespeare's *Julius Caesar.* Flavius has one scene at the start with Marullus, and one night Marullus, as usual, stood on a grey-painted beer crate to shout the line: 'Knew you not Pompey?' His long pants under his toga fell to the floor round the beer crate, trapping his feet. He could neither retrieve them nor get down from the beer crate. Olivier felt himself beginning to laugh uncontrollably, and got off the stage quickly, leaving Marullus to his fate. The unfortunate Marullus signalled desperately to the stage manager, who at last brought the curtain down. Olivier was fired the next day. He seems to have held this against Lena Ashwell, but it had been thoroughly unprofessional. Giggling on stage was a serious weakness for Olivier, not cured until he met Noel Coward.

Out of work again, he decided to see what old family friends could do. Unlike his famous contemporary John Gielgud, he did not come from a great theatrical family, though Gielgud's famous great-aunt, the legendary actress Ellen Terry, had once seen Olivier perform as a child and been impressed. But his father numbered among his friends one Canon Thorndike, whose daughter Sybil, now 43, was a major star and, with her husband Lewis Casson, a powerful manager. The previous year, in 1924, she had had a great triumph as St Joan, a part which Bernard Shaw wrote for her.

Olivier's first patrons Lewis Casson, Sybil Thorndike and G B Shaw

Thorndike and Casson took him on, Casson spelling out his duties: 'Spear, halberd and standard bearer, all the understudies you can undertake without looking ridiculous, and second assistant stage manager in *Henry VIII* at the Old Empire in Leicester Square,' all for £3 a week. Olivier pleaded for another £1, and got it in his second week.

He became very close to his two employers, who recognised quickly that they had hired an unusually gifted young actor. Sybil Thorndike became almost a substitute for the mother he had lost, and Lewis Casson a substitute for the father he never quite felt he had. And the company was far more prestigious that the one run by the once magnificent, but now slightly fading, Lena Ashwell. He enjoyed everything he did for Thorndike and Casson: stage management, spear-carrying, even working in the prompt box. He loved the cachet of being in distinguished theatrical company. The extra £1 made a huge difference to his life: new clothes, occasional meals at good restaurants. And he fell in love with the actress Angela Baddeley, who was happily married and cheerfully ignored both his advances and those of another young actor in the company, Carol Reed, later the director of films like *The Third Man* and *Oliver*.

It was a turning point. He was not yet a star, but by the time the run of *Henry VIII* ended, and with it Olivier's employment, in March 1926, he had another job to go to, playing a small but good part in *The Marvellous History of St Bernard* by Henri Gheon at the Birmingham Rep. Gheon was then a fashionable French religious dramatist who wore his Catholicism on his sleeve and wrote reverend plays about saints. Olivier, still a High Anglican, thought it *a beautiful parable play.*

The engagement was cut short by a national emergency. The general strike of May 1926 was triggered by the end of the government subsidy to the mineowners; for the mineowners' response was to demand longer hours for less pay from the miners. The miners' union leader Arthur Cook stomped the country with a simple message: 'Not a penny off the pay, not a minute on the day.'

Nothing defines the young Laurence Olivier more clearly than the side he chose. Along with many young men from comfortable homes, he chose to help break the strike. *Many members of the middle classes* he recalled languidly in his memoirs *helped to keep essential services going.* He went to work on the London Underground, first buying and putting on a fine pair of plus fours because he wanted to fit in and guessed, rightly, that *this would be almost a uniform among the volunteers.* Thus he fitted in with the other Hooray Henries who helped to ensure that the unions crawled back to work, defeated, after 12 days, and the mineowners were able to starve the miners into submission at their leisure over the winter. He would happily have done it for nothing – in fact, he expected to do it for nothing – but he found to his surprise and pleasure that the job brought him £5 a week. Never a man who thought deeply about politics, he was instinctively on the side of the class he sprang from, and remained so, writing serenely more than half a century later: *I have constantly been told in the last few years that I was on the wrong side and should be ashamed of myself.*

Once the strike ended, he did not remain long out of work. He toured with *The Farmer's Wife*, and while on tour he was introduced for the first time to the writings of the great director Konstantin Stanlislavsky. A copy of Stanislavsky's *My Life in Art* was passed round the company, and Olivier recorded that you could tell who was reading it from their behaviour. The actor who usually rushed through the stage door ten minutes before he was due to go on stage would start arriving an hour early, putting on makeup slowly and reflectively, wandering thoughtfully about the set touching everything, and refusing to take part in the back-stage chat. The book affected everything Olivier did after that, helping to make him not only a perfectionist but also an actor determined to live inside his character.

Konstantin Stanislavsky

After this he was taken on by the Birmingham Rep, where he worked from 1926 to 1928. It was another step up: he was part of the permanent company, he had many of the lead parts (though he had to play several small supporting parts as well), and the Birmingham Rep had a London outlet for some of its productions, the Royal Court Theatre in Sloane Square. He was well paid – £10 a week when not working, £15 when working normally, £20 for a lead part – and they even gave him the title role in *Uncle Vanya,* an extraordinary accolade since the character is supposed to be in his forties. In those days, a highly talented 19-year-old actor could get Uncle Vanya, yet had little chance of being cast as Romeo. In the actor-manager system, the great juvenile leads were generally reserved for the boss, who was always a lot older than Romeo is supposed to be. The theory was that these parts required greater maturity in performance than a 19-year-old could possibly possess. (The same, of course, could be said for Uncle Vanya.)

Stanislavsky's *My Life in Art* affected everything Olivier did, helping to make him not only a perfectionist but also an actor determined to live inside his character.

The actor-manager system was starting to decay in the 1920s, and the time was coming when this sort of age-blind casting would start to seem anachronistic to the point of being ludicrous. Ironically it was Olivier himself who gave the system a last outing in 1947, when at the age of 40 he cast himself as Hamlet, with an actress much younger than him playing Hamlet's mother Gertrude.

Laurence Olivier was a young man determined to succeed in his chosen profession, and applied himself single-mindedly and intelligently to that objective. When he heard that, in his second season with the Birmingham Rep, the production which was to go to London was *The Adding Machine* by American playwright Elmer Rice, he was at first distressed, because he only had a tiny part in it, but he decided to make something of it. He wangled an introduction to an American actress who taught him the East Side New York accent required. The rest of the cast, of course, had only a sufficiently good accent to satisfy a British audience. There were no American films or television shows in those days, and most people had only a rudimentary idea of what an American accent sounded like. Olivier's ploy worked – despite his small part, he was picked out for special praise by the *Observer* drama critic. And he had also learned a lesson which he remembered all his life: always make the effort to get the accent just right.

These two years brought Olivier into contact with two of the most important people in his life: his first wife Jill Esmond, and his lifelong friend and rival Ralph Richardson. He made a special effort to make a friend of Richardson, four years older than Olivier and a little better established. It started badly. Olivier was a little in awe of Richardson. Richardson was not sure he liked Olivier's growing friendship with Richardson's beautiful young wife, though there was nothing in it. But they discovered a shared dislike of old acting styles – they were part of the new move towards more naturalistic acting – and a shared taste for marathon drinking sessions in the local pub. Richardson's wife was also in the company – Muriel Hewitt, a young actress with whom, apparently, most male members of the company, including Olivier, were hopelessly in love. She, as Angela Baddeley had done, ignored his advances. Peggy Ashcroft also gently spurned him.

A publicity shot of the newlyweds: Olivier and Jill Esmond

So he turned his attentions to another actress, Jill Esmond. He was desperate for those carnal pleasures which were forbidden by his strict religion until his wedding night. She was serious, a little aloof, attractive rather than pretty, sexually shy and inexperienced but professionally, at that time, rather more established than Olivier, and a member of a theatrical dynasty, with parents who were both major theatrical figures.

It took two years to get her to agree to marry him – hardly surprising perhaps, since the nicest thing he was able to say about her in his memoirs was that, though not dazzlingly attractive, *she would most certainly do excellent well for a wife*, and that he wasn't likely to do any better at his age (which was 21) and with his relatively undistinguished career. He seems to have applied the same cold calculation to his first marriage as he applied to his career.

He planned his next career opportunity equally carefully. In those days, when theatres could not open on Sunday, London theatre managements found imaginative ways of using the space. The Strand, run by a left-wing actor-manager, Arthur Bourchier, ran socialist propaganda meetings. Others ran Sunday Play Societies, at which a play was tried out in front of an audience of society members, which made it legal, for it was not a performance open to the public. Actors were not paid, but the societies provided showcases for their talents, since audiences generally included influential producers, managers and agents.

So in 1928, Olivier jumped at the chance to play Captain Stanhope at a Sunday theatre society production of R C Sherriff's *Journey's End*, set in the trenches of the First World War, even though he did not like the play much. He had heard that Basil Dean was looking for someone to play the title part of the Foreign Legion hero in P C Wren's *Beau Geste*. After his Sunday performance at the Apollo Theatre, Dean went straight to Olivier's dressing room and offered him the part.

As it turned out, Olivier would have done far better to stick with *Journey's End*, which was a fabulous success and would have made his name. It was a remarkable early misjudgement. This was partly because Olivier, who was 11 when the First World War ended and, unusually, seems to have lost no one close to him in the fighting, never quite understood the lasting resonance the war had for many of his generation, especially for those just five or so years older than him. R C Sherriff had poured his hatred of war, his bitter memories of the trenches, into his play, which is still considered one of the great war plays. For many of his fellow citizens, who understood these things all too well, it made no sense to watch the traumas and hardships of the French Foreign Legion in *Beau Geste*, when they had the greatest of all war traumas of their own, close and sharp in everyone's memories, to put on the stage. For more aware people than Olivier, *Journey's End* was a crucial part of the process of coming to terms with the horrors of the Great War.

But he was stuck with *Beau Geste*. Basil Dean was a martinet of a producer, bullying female members of the cast and forcing his male actors through a punishing two-hour exercise class every morning, followed by a hour's marching, eight hours' rehearsal and an hour singing martial songs. After all that it still managed to fail completely, and so did Olivier's next seven plays. But the harsh critical notices often remarked that the production had one saving grace. 'Mr Olivier gets out of bad parts all the charm there is in them' wrote the critic James Agate. Young Laurence Olivier was a huge talent, they agreed.

He was now a young man with the dashing good looks of a matinee idol, a fashionable Ronald Colman moustache grown for *Journey's End* and nurtured for *Beau Geste*, enormous actorish charm (he behaved in the way that would today get him called a luvvy) and, most important of all, boundless and impatient ambition. The critics were right. Laurence Olivier could afford the odd mistake. He was on his way.

After two years of this, in 1930 Olivier's career looked up again. First he was offered two roles in the infant British film industry, and despite the snobbish contempt British actors tended to show for the cinema at that time, he jumped at the work because he needed the money. Then, crucially, Noel Coward invited him to his Belgravia home and handed him a typed script. It was *Private Lives*, about a divorced couple who meet on honeymoon with new spouses (and, of course, realise they are still in love with each other). The two were to be played by himself and his friend Gertrude Lawrence, and Coward wanted Olivier for Gertrude Lawrence's new husband.

A star turn. Olivier with Adrianne Allen, Noel Coward and Gertrude Lawrence in *Private Lives*

Olivier disliked the part but recognised Coward as a man he could learn from. He also recognised that Coward's offer of £50 a week was as good as he was likely to get anywhere. Coward rather brutally but effectively cured Olivier of his tendency to burst out giggling on stage. 'I'm going to do everything in my power to make you giggle and corpse at every performance' he told him. When Coward stopped, Gertrude Lawrence would start, and if he succumbed, he would be reprimanded backstage in front of the entire company. 'If nine months of that treatment does not knock this amateurish smear on your otherwise bright new talent out of you, then you'd really better start brushing up on some other trade.'

They opened in Edinburgh, then in the brand-new Phoenix Theatre in London's West End, and Olivier experienced for the first time the thrill of being in a West End hit. After three months they went to New York, where Jill Esmond took over the part of Olivier's new wife.

He was now a star, and starting to be well off. In New York he started a regular love affair with the Algonquin Hotel, which persisted all his life. Until 1929, the year before Olivier discovered it, the Algonquin was the headquarters of the circle of writers and literati around Dorothy Parker, and for years anyone from the British theatre who could afford it stayed there in New York.

But another love affair must have seemed more important at the time, though it was far less enduring. Jill Esmond had at last consented to marry him. Born in London in 1908, the year after Olivier, she was the daughter of a playwright and actor, H V Esmond (who died before Olivier met his daughter), and a well-known actress, Eva Moore, and because her parents had to spend a lot of time on tour, was sent to boarding school from the age of five.

He pursued her with relentless devotion. She was frank, straightforward, direct and independent. This must have been the sort of woman he wanted at the time – it was only later that he started to yearn for the more ethereal, clinging qualities of a Vivien Leigh. Before the wedding she gave an interview (she was by now well known enough for this to be the sort of theatrical marriage to interest the newspapers) to the left-wing *Daily Herald* in which she said: 'Victorian girls must have looked forward to marriage as a partial escape from a domestic cage. Today marriage is in some ways more like an entrance into a cage.' To another journalist she had once said: 'I don't expect marriage to be one long dream. One settles down on an even keel, a mutual adjustment. I should certainly have friends and secrets unknown to a husband of mine.' She was something of a mentor to Olivier, making him get his crooked teeth sorted out, clipping his thick eyebrows, making him style his hair in the film-star fashion of the twenties. She was, in short, going to be a thoroughly independent sort of wife, one who would not allow herself to be treated as anything less than an equal – and perhaps, in the end, that did not suit Olivier.

There was a little family problem of the sort that seems absurd now. Eva Moore wanted her daughter to be married in the Chapel Royal, Savoy, where she had herself been married. The Revd

A formal wedding photograph of Olivier and Jill Esmond

Gerard Olivier tersely vetoed this. He could not, he said, enter the Chapel Royal 'as it is known that divorced people are able to be married there.' Jill's mother was deeply distressed, but the Reverend won, as bigots generally do, and the wedding took place in Olivier's old haunt, All Saints, and was conducted by the vicar who was still there from his days in its choir. Olivier, as he candidly admitted, was never able to answer back to his father. Eva behaved well nonetheless, providing a splendid reception. They had a splendid wedding day. But the wedding night in Lulworth Cove was dreadful.

The Revd Gerard Olivier tersely vetoed this. He could not, he said, enter the Chapel Royal 'as it is known that divorced people are able to be married there.'

The drive took much longer than they expected. Olivier describes in his memoirs what happened when they got there; it makes one of the frankest and most entertaining descriptions of the agonies which young people who have 'saved themselves' until their wedding day are likely to go through.

We had been most kindly lent a lovely house by Lady Fripp, a friend of Eva's, whose generous inclinations did not stop there; no doubt with the kindest intentions in the world, she left us also her two sweet, but agonisingly embarrassed, grown-up, single, young daughters as hostesses for the occasion. This made a signal addition to the bride and groom's already mounting embarrassment . . .

The two sweet Fripp girls served us supper and toyed with something on their own plates as well. None of us was capable of dealing with the degree of agonised shyness that was reached at the end of that meal. Finally, Jill and I both dived at something of the order of 'Well, now . . . er . . . p'raps it's time we went up to our room and . . . er . . . unpacked . . . ?'

I have never been able to think of that slightly pagan festivity referred to as the honeymoon as anything but disastrous, and I am sure that Jill has always felt the same. After some hesitant efforts to accomplish

something we hoped would pass for foreplay – my own efforts, I knew,
would not pass muster in a third floor back room in Lisle Street, and all
that would rest in my bride's memory would be an endurance test – at last
we turned away from each other.

The marriage never recovered from this disastrous start. It was,
eventually, consummated, though that took quite a long time.
Olivier claims Jill had told him before the wedding that she did
not love him, but he had hoped to change her mind once they were
married; after Lulworth Cove there seemed little chance of that.
They did, of course, learn to make love, and no doubt to enjoy it,
but that brought another crisis for Olivier. Jill did not want to
have children – but to the Reverend Gerard Olivier and his son,
contraception was as short a road to hell as marrying a divorcee.
Since his main purpose in marrying was to have sex, what was
Olivier to do? He did the sensible thing. He practised contraception and stopped going to church. After that, his father's High
Anglicanism, until then central to his life, simply faded out of it.

It's impossible to leave this rather sad first marriage without
mentioning what at the time was unmentionable. Olivier was
bisexual – and Jill Esmond was discovering that she was a lesbian.
It's likely that the heterosexual side of him was stronger, but it's
perfectly possible that the homosexual side was really dominant,
and was repressed. It would have horrified the father he dreaded,
offended against his religion, and quite possibly brought him a
prison term. No wonder he repressed it.

The 1920s was a comparatively liberated decade. Though
homosexuality was, of course, illegal, it did not carry quite the
stigma that it had carried before the war, and there were several
men in the theatre whose homosexuality was known in theatrical
circles, but never written about.

One of these was Olivier's friend Noel Coward. Witty and
patrician, eight years older than Olivier, Coward had been writing, producing and acting since he was 12, and had an unbounded

Noel Coward aboard ship at Southampton

(and generally entirely justified) belief in his own abilities. He found Olivier generally not widely read apart from parts he had played, and handed him a reading list of novels and poetry he considered essential. Olivier found it easy to take direction from Coward, whom he respected. According to Coward's friend and biographer Cole Lesley, 'Noel adored Larry, there's no other word for it.' Coward probably also knew, or at least suspected, the truth about Jill Esmond's sexuality.

And it is to Coward that Olivier is referring when he writes in his memoirs, with almost painful reticence, of *the one male with whom some sexual dalliance had not been loathsome for me to contemplate.* Coward was the man whom he *had felt it desperately necessary to warn* that Olivier had old-fashioned *ideals which must not be trodden underfoot and destroyed.* Though at St Edwards he had been *unfairly labelled . . . as the school tart* he felt *that the homosexual act would be a step darkly destructive to my soul.* Yet – to guess at the meaning of two more long paragraphs of coy, overblown, elliptical prose – he had a jolly good time having sex with Noel.

John Gielgud to the rescue

Noel Coward, seven years older than Olivier, was more than the instrument of forbidden pleasures. He was a mentor and friend. Coward's cure for Olivier's giggling was just one of the ways in which Olivier learned from his professionalism. He also educated him socially. 'Coward' writes one of Olivier's least friendly biographers, Roger Lewis 'consolidated what Jill and her social connections had begun, introducing him into a glamorous world of luncheons, first nights and supper parties . . . "You can never live too well, my dears" Coward announced. "When you live well people want to know you."'

But Coward's advice was sometimes ignored. During the Broadway run of *Private Lives*, a Hollywood talent scout saw Olivier and Jill Esmond, and offered them both contracts. Coward thought Hollywood was a dreadful idea, and tried to talk his protégé out of it, but unsuccessfully. The American studio system appalled most British actors who went to Hollywood at that time, and Olivier was no exception. It was brutal and exploitative, and dispiriting to a perfectionist like Olivier, for you often had to shoot a scene without a detailed knowledge what had happened to your character earlier in the film. It must have seemed the exact opposite of those inspiring lessons he had picked up from Stanislavsky's book. He made three forgotten and, by all accounts (including his own) forgettable, films in two years, comforting himself with the knowledge that he was being handsomely paid. It was the beginning of the Great Depression, and he more than once started a film only to have it closed down by the financiers with terrifying suddenness.

But he had a whale of a time, touring the bars with Douglas Fairbanks Junior, sniffing cocaine (once only, according to Fairbanks), and starting to make up for his disappointment with Jill by spending nights with two of his co-stars.

After two years he found that Hollywood had no further plans for him, and he wanted to go home, where he had an offer to do a film at Ealing Studios (another turkey, as it turned out), but Jill had been made an offer she thought she couldn't refuse, a chance of real stardom in a David Selznick film. They had an understanding, as many actor couples do, that if their work forced them to be apart, so be it. But Olivier persuaded her to go home with him.

There are conflicting stories about exactly what happened, but her certainly told her, and perhaps believed, that Selznick was stringing Jill along; he intended stardom, and the part he was promising Jill, for Katherine Hepburn, not Jill. She was never quite convinced of this, and it looks as though he urged, rather unfairly, that her place was by her husband. Their son Tarquin says: 'He forced her to turn down her big break.' At any rate, after days of indecision, she agreed to go to London with him.

Perhaps she quickly regretted and resented her decision; in any case, it was clear to Douglas Fairbanks Junior and his wife Joan Crawford that the Olivier marriage was in trouble. Jill's mother never forgave Olivier; she thought he had ruined her daughter's big chance of stardom. And it can hardly have improved her temper when she heard that, despite everything, her son-in-law had suddenly picked himself up and taken himself back to Hollywood. This time he, rather than Jill, had an offer he couldn't refuse – to play opposite Greta Garbo in *Queen Christina*.

It didn't last. He was fired after a fortnight. Garbo didn't like him, and perhaps he was too much in awe of her. He was handsomely paid off, did not allow his hurt pride to lead him into burning more bridges than necessary, and went with Jill on holiday in Hawaii for a fortnight to get over it. Next came a play in New York for him and Jill, then back to London, where they had their Chelsea house decorated by a decorator who was fashionable among theatre people, *a sweet old puss* according to Olivier, in an over-the-top fashion, with massive white silk curtains, massive furniture, newly-carved oak, tapestries on the walls, and a chained ring-tailed lemur called Tony in the minstrel's gallery. Despite, or perhaps because of, what he still regarded as a deprived childhood, Olivier was taking to the star lifestyle like a duck to water. Noel Coward was horrified, complaining of Olivier's 'delusions of grandeur.'

At that time no one thought of Olivier as a Shakespearian actor. Jack Hawkins, who was, thought Olivier's idea that he might one day play Hamlet was rather ridiculous. He 'just didn't have the voice.' He had been away from the London stage for too long: he was remembered vaguely as a nice-looking, competent performer, one of many available to a West End producer, and none of his most recent West End shows had been especially successful. He and Jill were not especially happy together, nor were they especially unhappy. By 1933, when he had finally accepted he could not change her lesbianism, he started to get depressed.

The next job was in London, under Coward's direction again, in what Olivier thought was a fine play, which flopped. Olivier was treading water. That was about to change.

This time the instrument of change was his own contemporary, an actor about as different from Olivier as was possible, but with whom he had one of the longest and most fruitful professional relationships of his life: John Gielgud, who by 1934 was already what Olivier was to become, an established Shakespearian actor.

Gielgud was to direct *Queen of Scots*, a play by Gordon Daviot about Mary Queen of Scots, with himself and Gwen Ffangcon-Davies in the lead parts, and a splendid cast including the young James Mason. He had cast Ralph Richardson as the arrogant,

John Gielgud in *Hamlet*

passionate, brawling, flashy philanderer Bothwell, but it became painfully clear in rehearsals that Richardson was not comfortable in the part, especially in the love scenes with Gwen Ffangcon-Davies. Less than a fortnight before opening night, Richardson asked Gielgud to release him from the contract, and suggested his old chum Larry Olivier for the part instead.

Gielgud hardly knew Olivier, but had seen him on stage and admired his physicality. Olivier was over the moon, as Richardson knew he would be, at the chance to play a big costume role, and took his cloak home to wear at weekends. The Stanislavsky readings had not been forgotten. Gielgud rehearsed with him for 14 hours a day to be ready for the opening night. The play was not entirely successful, despite the usual rave reviews for Gielgud, and Olivier's performance had a mixed reception, but, half unnoticed, a great theatrical partnership had been born.

Another Gielgud production made their partnership a legend. It happened almost by accident. After *Queen of Scots* Olivier did some more film work, and more on the London stage. He also briefly became a producer-director, a new breed which was starting to replace the pre-war actor-manager. What had happened was that, by the mid 1930s, an actor-manager who raised the money, leased the theatre, found the cast, directed the play, was no longer a viable way of working because theatrical entrepreneurs were mostly financiers or businessmen – 'angels' as they came to be called. And new productions required much more direction than the old actor-managers provided: lighting and other technical matters were more complicated, and greater realism demanded more of the director. The result was the rise of the producer-director, who had a much more hands-on role as a director than the actor-manager, but was much less concerned with administration, finance and the booking of theatres. This was the role Olivier assumed for a play called *Golden Arrow*.

By the mid 1930s, an actor-manager who raised the money, leased the theatre, found the cast, directed the play, was no longer a viable way of working because theatrical entrepreneurs were mostly financiers or businessmen – 'angels' as they came to be called.

Then John Gielgud was forced to abandon at short notice a production he had intended to stage at the New Theatre, and with just three weeks rehearsal time, he decided to do *Romeo and Juliet*. He thought that each generation needed to rediscover Shakespeare for itself, and he wanted to treat *R&J* 'as though it were a modern work which has never been produced before.'

The great innovation which made it one of the defining events of inter-war theatre was equally accidental. There are conflicting versions of exactly how it happened, but what we know is this. Gielgud was worried about taking on Romeo himself – partly because of the burden this would place on him, in the short time available, if he was to play Romeo and direct as well. He decided to play Mercutio, whose early death would give him more time to rehearse his cast, and his first thought for Romeo was his old friend Robert Donat; he turned to Olivier in despair when Donat explained that he was already committed.

Olivier too had doubts – he said he had thought of staging the play himself, with Jill Esmond. But he would not have got many backers. Gielgud was an established Shakespearean actor;

Olivier was not. Gielgud, for his part, was not at all easy in his mind about it, thinking Olivier far too coarse, with an insufficient respect for the cadences of Shakespeare's verse. This was at least partly why Gielgud hit on the idea of having himself as Mercutio and Olivier as Romeo for six weeks, then reversing these roles: as an insurance policy, lest Olivier failed to make a successful Romeo.

But as an unintentional publicity stunt, it was brilliant, for it drew the critics to see the production a second time. Gielgud's direction was widely praised, and so was Peggy Ashcroft's Juliet. But the differing styles of Gielgud and Olivier puzzled critics, and it continued to do so for half a century, for as long as both men were alive and working. It was in *R&J* that Gielgud and Olivier emerged as the leaders of two different and opposing movements in British theatre.

John Gielgud, three years older than Olivier, was steeped in theatre. His mother came from the great theatrical Terry dynasty. The greatest of many famous relatives was his great-aunt Ellen Terry, Britain's greatest classical actress in the second half of the nineteenth century and Gielgud's childhood idol. His great-uncle Fred Terry was one of the great Victorian actor-managers, working with his wife Julia Neilson. Their children, Phyllis and Dennis Neilson-Terry, were already established actors in the 1920s. The Terrys, according to Gielgud's biographer Jonathan Croall, had 'large appetites, gracious manners, fine voices and beautiful diction, but also a flamboyant temperament, great stamina and an enormous capacity for hard work,' all of which were to characterise the whole of John Gielgud's long life. One of Ellen Terry's illegitimate children (she led a scandalous life by Victorian standards) was Gordon Craig, an eminent theatre designer and theoretician.

Gielgud's father's parents had come to Britain from Lithuania and Poland at the start of the nineteenth century, and one great grandparent had been a leading Lithuanian actress. It was a reasonably well-off Victorian family, happier and more fun than the spartan, God-fearing home run by the Reverend Gerard Olivier. But his vocation was never in doubt; for, as he once said himself, 'If your great-aunt happens to be Ellen Terry, your great-uncle Fred Terry, your cousins Gordon Craig and Phyllis Neilson-Terry, and your grandmother the greatest Shakespearean actress in all Lithuania, you are hardly likely to drift into the fish trade.'

The young John Gielgud

Gielgud was delicate and mannered, without any of Olivier's physicality. He spoke Shakespeare in the classical manner, concentrating on doing full justice to the poetry, the music of the words. Olivier, on the other hand, saw Shakespeare's words as the means by which the character was conveyed: he wanted to be Romeo, not to act him, and he saw Romeo as a hot-blooded adolescent seething with sexual tension. It was a clash of styles, and Gielgud as director tried without success to rein in his leading man. 'Larry', one cast member told Jonathan Croall, 'was out to dominate the play by the sheer force of his presence, to ride roughshod over the rest of us as we went about doing things in our rather restrained Gielgudian fashion.' Gielgud put it this way: 'I bullied him a great deal about his verse-speaking, which, he admitted himself, he wasn't happy about.' A Gielgud protégé, Alec Guinness, has said: 'We all admired John greatly, but we were not so keen on

We all admired John greatly (in Romeo and Juliet), but we were not so keen on Larry. He seemed a bit cheap and vulgar, striving after effects and making nonsense of the verse.

Alec Guinness.

Larry. He seemed a bit cheap and vulgar, striving after effects and making nonsense of the verse.'

And you can sense exactly the same events being described in Olivier's own interesting if slightly self-serving analysis. The public, he wrote years later in his book *On Acting*, just wanted verse spoken beautifully, so *I was the outsider and John was the jewel; and a shining one too, deservedly so. John still {in 1986} has the most beautiful voice, but I felt in those days he allowed it to dominate his performances and, if he was lost for a moment, he would dive straight back into its honey . . . He was giving the familiar tradition fresh life, whereas I was completely disregarding the old in favour of something new . . . I think I was right, and I know that John will go on thinking that he was.*

The critics turned out in force when the two exchanged roles, and most preferred Gielgud's Romeo, more traditional, poetic, tender and musical. Olivier was much cast down by the reviews. Only St John Irvine in the *Observer* seemed ready to embrace his new style: 'I have seen few sights so moving as the spectacle of Mr Olivier's Romeo . . . [Shakespeare's] eyes would have shone had he seen this Romeo, young and ardent and full of clumsy grace.'

As time went on, Olivier's style began to prevail. People started to point out that you could really believe Romeo's physical passion for Juliet when Olivier did the balcony scene. Gielgud, though poetic and romantic, was never quite sensual enough. Even Gielgud himself started to envy his rival's physicality, and to be generous about his verse-speaking – more generous than Olivier was able to be about Gielgud's performance. And the critics raved about Olivier's Mercutio, with its swagger and its sarcasm. But despite all that, Olivier never quite forgave Gielgud.

Which was better? You can never recreate what happens in a

theatre. The curtain comes down, and it's gone, living only in the memories of those who saw it. There is probably not a soul left alive today who saw Olivier and Gielgud playing Romeo and Mercutio. What we can be sure of is that Olivier represented the future – as, eventually, Gielgud himself generously acknowledged. 'His new approach to the verse' writes one of Olivier's biographers, Donald Spoto, 'signalled a stylistic turning point in playing Shakespeare.' Shakespeare on the English stage would never again be declaimed, as it had been in the nineteenth century by Sir Henry Irving and Gielgud's famous Terry ancestors.

The show was a tremendous success, running for 186 performances at the New Theatre, the longest continuous run of *Romeo and Juliet* on record, and showed that Shakespeare could still be a paying proposition in the West End, even in the 1930s.

But Gielgud and Olivier never appeared on stage together again. During the run, Olivier's new-found reputation as a Shakespearean actor led to an invitation to film *As You Like It* with Elisabeth Bergner, which, despite his misgivings and despite the strain of filming during the day and performing on stage at night, he took for the money, £600 a week for two months – a fortune in those days. It was not a success, mainly because Bergner was hopelessly miscast as Rosalind.

Olivier now embarked on management himself for the first time. He, Ralph Richardson and playwright J B Priestley put up the money between them to stage Priestley's *Bees on the Boat Deck* at the Lyric Theatre. It was not a success and came off after a month, losing its three backers a small sum of money. Olivier swiftly recouped his share in an Alexander Korda film called *Fire Over England.* In this otherwise unremarkable swashbuckler, Olivier worked for the first time with Vivien Leigh.

By then, they were an item. Vivien was born in 1913 in Darjeeling, India, and deposited in a south London convent at the age of six. She felt she had been abandoned, especially when her

Absolutely ravishing: photo portraits of Vivien Leigh as her stage career began

parents did not even take her away for the summer holidays. A nun gave her a cat to hold when there was no one around, and she claimed later that that cat had kept her sane. She grew up amid Catholic threats of hellfire and feeling unloved: her demands for affection and sex as an adult are surely not hard to understand.

A sophisticated education in several European schools left the clever and magically beautiful teenager fluent in French and German and with obvious acting talent that took her to the Royal Academy of Dramatic Art, which she left before her year's training was over to marry a wealthy lawyer called Leigh Holman. In 1933, when she was 19, their daughter Suzanne was born. She signed with a theatrical agent, took her husband's first name to make a stage name of Vivien Leigh, and became an instant minor West End success in a play called *The Mask of Virtue*.

She and Olivier got to know each other originally in the company of their respective spouses, Jill Esmond and Leigh Holman. Their furtive affair began after Vivien visited Olivier's dressing room during the run of *R&J*. It was not really a secret. Theatrical

London knew what was going on, and so, almost certainly, did Jill Esmond and Leigh Holman. Both were used to their spouse's infidelities: Jill Esmond probably knew about Olivier's occasional one night stands with his leading ladies in Hollywood, and Leigh Holman may well not have missed the rumours connecting Vivien to Alexander Korda and to John Buckmaster. So too did many members of their audiences; they often did not approve, and sometimes showed it with the occasional boo from the gallery. Olivier took a rather strange comfort from the fact that, during this period, the Queen – the wife of King George VI – came to see one of his performances, as Othello; he apparently feared that his shocking private life would prevent such royal recognition.

I soon began to feel sorry for Jill, indeed to feel pain for her and, of course, guilt he wrote in his memoirs. *But this thing was as fatally irresistible for us . . .* Sometimes Olivier writes with the self-indulgence of an Edwardian melodrama. Later his memoirs record: *We could not keep from touching each other, making love almost within Jill's vision. This welding closeness tripped the obvious decision, and two marriages were severed.*

Years after Olivier's death, his and Jill's son Tarquin Olivier told the world that when he was being born, his father hurried home 'with Vivien's scent all over him.' As a child, he kept by his bed a picture of Olivier in armour as Henry V because 'I was determined to have a father.' Olivier never managed to have much of a relationship with Tarquin – not because Jill prevented him, for she did not, but because there always seemed to be something more important for him to do. He made the effort when his son was an undergraduate, but it was probably too late. Tarquin says his father 'never acknowledged the platform my mother gave him.' In those early days, Jill was the star with the brilliant future. 'It was my mother who gave his career lift-off in films and in the theatre' says Tarquin. 'She introduced him to so many people, like Noel Coward, Rudyard Kipling. She negotiated his fees.

She was getting the work, he was not. She was doing much better in Hollywood than he was.'

Jill Esmond was sensible and thoughtful, and always treated Olivier as though she were the senior partner, offering him her frank appraisal of his work, based not only on her own considerable knowledge, but a long family history in the theatre. Vivien was completely different: ethereal, theatrical, beautiful and magical. Unlike Jill she did not aspire to an equal relationship with him; she hero-worshipped Olivier, he basked in her admiration, and one suspects he was for the first time experiencing the sexual and emotional obsession which is often known as being in love.

Once she was sure the thing was inevitable, Jill Esmond sensibly bent her mind to making sure she and her son were well looked after financially. Since Leigh Holman was in no more hurry to give his errant spouse a divorce than Jill Esmond was, it took three years to tie up all the loose ends, and Larry and Vivien married in 1940. Olivier seems always to have resented Jill, taking his revenge by revealing in his memoirs that they never loved each other and complaining in old age: *Jill saw me as a meal ticket for life.* She certainly felt betrayed, and felt too that he had repaid rather miserably all the help given to him by the Esmond family at the start of his career. She hardly worked after the divorce, and she never married again, living with Tarquin and a succession of female companions – first Robert Donat's estranged wife Ella Voysey, and later, for many years, her closest friend, Joy Pearce.

Olivier's memoirs make no mention of the crucial fact that, as a little boy, Tarquin developed meningitis, and was expected either to die young or to grow up permanently handicapped, which is why, during the war, his mother took him to the USA, because the noise of bombs might do him great damage. 'Jill, rather surprisingly, has been a wonderful mother to Tarquin' wrote Noel Coward, who was Tarquin's godfather, in his diary 'and he geuinely adores her. Larry, as a father figure, has not come off quite so well.' Jill Esmond died in 1990, aged 82.

She may have thought him weak, but she also thought him a genius, and did not grieve over her own lost career if it had been sacrificed on the altar of what she considered a greater talent than hers or anyone else's. 'I was always conscious that his potential was enormous. I always knew he was the much more important person' she once said. It's impossible, since we cannot see her on stage, to assess what she might have been had she not met Olivier; but many people who did see her work thought she might have become a big star, and that she subordinated her career to his.

Thanks to John Gielgud, Olivier was at last established as a classical actor. He could have followed up his venture with Richardson and Priestley by becoming a West End actor-manager, or he could have followed up *Fire over England* by seeking his fortune in film. He made instead a conscious choice to accept Tyrone Guthrie's invitation to work for £20 a week doing classical theatre at the Old Vic. He had been introduced to Guthrie by Jill Esmond's mother – the last of many contributions the Esmond family made to his early career. He started with Hamlet, his first shot at what he always considered the greatest and most challenging of all Shakespeare's great tragic figures. Vivien was also to be in the Old Vic company, and to play Ophelia opposite Olivier's Hamlet.

The Old Vic was a splendid theatre built on reclaimed marshland in 1818 which for many years had offered melodrama and farce, but which after 1914 began to offer a famous cycle of Shakespeare plays. Guthrie's invitation confirmed Olivier's status: there were few actors who would turn down an invitation to enhance their reputations at the Old Vic, for a fraction of the salary they could earn elsewhere. For the 29-year-old Olivier it was a heaven-sent opportunity. And it was made sweeter for him by the fact that John Gielgud was also to play Hamlet – their performances, like their Romeos, would alternate at the Old Vic.

He was still a man on a mission. Other actors, like Gielgud, spoke Shakespeare as verse, but Olivier spoke it as dialogue. His Hamlet was noisy and exciting. There was what Michael Billington describes as 'a famous leap, after the play scene, from the perched up throne to the mimic stage below, and thence down to the footlights: a typical piece of Olivier bravura almost designed to highlight the difference between himself and the nobly lyrical but more physically inhibited Gielgud.' More than once he was hurt in the duel with Laertes, played by Michael Redgrave, for he had typically insisted that Redgrave should lunge violently at him.

In preparation for the part he and Guthrie visited, not only an eminent Shakespearean scholar, but also a psychiatrist, Professor Ernest Jones, who told him he was sure Hamlet suffered from an Oedipus complex. *The Oedipus complex*, Olivier concluded, *can claim responsibility for a formidable share of all that is wrong with him.* The same might perhaps be said of Olivier himself. Certainly Vivien Leigh thought so, and was convinced that in rehearsing the part, Olivier was confronting his feelings over the early death of his own mother. In any event, it explained Hamlet's 'weakness for dramatics' which 'would be reasonable if the dramatics spurred him to action, but unfortunately they help to delay it. It is as if his shows of temperament not only exhaust him but give him relief from his absorption in his purpose.'

It was a successful Hamlet, which, together with Vivien's adoration, revived Olivier's battered self-confidence. He frequently made announcements at the end of the performance on behalf of the cast. On 30 January 1937 he stepped forward and told them: 'Ladies and gentlemen, tonight a great actress has been born. Laertes has a daughter.' Michael Redgrave's child was christened Vanessa.

But he overstepped himself when the Old Vic company was asked, by the Danish Tourist Board, to take its *Hamlet* to Elsinore, the castle where the play is set. Olivier demanded that the actress playing Ophelia, Cherry Cottrell, should be replaced by Vivien. Guthrie refused, Vivien scalded Olivier with her hysterical fury, and Olivier returned to Guthrie and seemed to imply that if the change was not made, he would not go. Guthrie gave in. Cherry Cottrell was devastated. It was, she rightly pointed out, about as unprofessional as you can get. What Vivien's Ophelia was like, we shall never know. Reports of it from the rest of the cast suggest it was immature and unconvincing, and it is impossible to tell how far this is due to their understandable resentment at the way she got the part.

After Hamlet came Sir Toby Belch in *Twelfth Night*, which he played as a comic buffon, with Jill as Maria. It premiered just as *Fire Over England* was being released. Then came *Henry V*.

Seven years later, when Olivier was to film *Henry V*, Britain was on the road to a wartime victory, and you could make the most of the heroic, almost triumphalist tone of the play. But in 1937 most people still hoped against hope that Prime Minister Neville Chamberlain could somehow avert war in Europe. When, the next year, Chamberlain returned from a Munich conference with Hitler, Mussolini and French Premier Edouard Daladier and talked of 'peace in our time', he was responding to the deepest desires of British people.

Olivier did not think much about politics – in retrospect he saw the Munich agreement as 'only a postponement, as between a try-out and a London production.' But he was a master at sensing a public mood. So he was wary of doing *Henry V*, being, as he put it in his memoirs, 'influenced by the 1930s dislike of all heroism.' In rehearsal he seemed uncharacteristically shy of the play's bombast. His friend and mentor Ralph Richardson told him to 'glory in it' and his director Tyrone Guthrie complained about his delivery of the famous speech before the battle. 'And gentlemen in England now abed/ Shall think themselves accursed they were not here/ And hold their manhoods cheap while any speaks/ That fought with us upon St Crispin's Day.' Olivier was saying this quietly and gravely. Guthrie exploded: 'It's too disappointing for your audience, you're taking all the thrill out of the play, and for heaven's sake that's all it's got.' They cajoled him into the buccaneering performance which he repeated for the camera four years later. The result was a performance that somehow embodied English nationalism – which was fine by Olivier, who was rather simplistically patriotic, but was not what he had intended.

Next came a delightful French holiday with Vivien – they were confirmed Francophiles – down a route which Charles Laughton mapped out for them, and which has since gone into the guidebooks as 'la route gastronomique': Avalon, Auxerre, Dijon, Beaune, Macon, Vienne, Montelimar. They strayed a little to visit the town of Nay, from which the last of Olivier's Huguenot ancestors left for England in 1685. It was followed, for both of them, by a couple of unremarkable films for Alexander Korda.

They bought a home together, Durham Cottage, a splendid seventeenth-century house in Chelsea, which Vivien decorated with exquisite taste and no consideration at all for expense, and they invited Ralph Richardson and Meriel Forbes, who was to become Richardson's second wife, to dinner on Guy Fawkes night, which happened also to be Vivien's birthday. It turned out to be a dreadful evening which tells us a good deal about both Olivier and Richardson.

They gave Richardson a bottle of champagne and told him there was plenty more, because the other three considered that they could appreciate the fine Burgundy Olivier had provided, but it would be wasted on Ralph. Richardson got very drunk and produced the box of fireworks he had brought. Olivier suggested he take them outside, but Richardson said 'Oh, my dear fellow' and gave Olivier's face a playful slap – *he always slapped one's face much too hard, I thought* wrote Olivier when telling the story in *On Acting*. Then he started letting off his fireworks on the dining room window sill, scarring it with huge burns; then he nailed a catherine wheel to one of Laurence and Vivien's favourite trees; then he stuck them on the mantelpiece. Realising rather late that he had given offence, he grabbed his wife's hand and said: 'Come on, Mu, best leave these people.' He burst through the French windows, breaking the lock and the glass, stepped into the pond, knocked over one of Vivien's favourite statues, broke through a newly planted hedge of lilac, broke the handle on the front gate, and was gone.

Back at the Old Vic, *Macbeth* was next on the menu. It was Olivier's first go at it, and was not entirely successful. Olivier put this down to the highly stylised direction by Michel St Denis, but it was at least as much the fault of his own over-preparation. Always a stickler for makeup, he overdid it this time. Vivien Leigh said wittily: 'You hear Macbeth's first line, then Larry's makeup comes on, then Banquo comes on, then Larry comes on.' Nonetheless, reviews were good and it was commercially successful.

Then came *Othello*. Olivier and Guthrie once again went to sit at the feet of Professor Ernest Jones, coming back convinced that Iago was subconsciously in love with Othello and had to destroy him. The problem was that Ralph Richardson, fresh from his adventures with fireworks in Olivier's home, was playing Othello to Olivier's Iago, and Richardson was almost aggressively heterosexual – macho, we might say today. Some years previously, in his Birmingham Rep days, when Olivier first got to know Richardson, he made a rather fey joke, and instantly worried that Richardson would be offended by it. Richardson was not a man who would take kindly to the suggestion that Olivier should camp up Iago a bit.

Nonetheless, Olivier and Guthrie tried to sell him the idea. Once, in rehearsals, Olivier threw his arms round Richardson and kissed him full on the lips. Richardson coolly disengaged himself, murmuring 'There, there, now; dear boy; good boy.' Another time, when Othello is having a paroxysm and Iago was to fall to the ground beside him, Olivier lay there and simulated an orgasm, but the actress Athene Seyler saw him do it in rehearsal and said: 'I'm sure I have no idea what you were up to when you threw yourself on the ground beside Ralph.' So Olivier and Guthrie gave up, and let Iago simply hate Othello because Othello was black and his superior. Today the story only leaves us with the intriguing, but unanswerable question: in this production, was Iago subconsciously in love with his Othello?

Maybe; for as soon as the Old Vic run was over, a film offer came Olivier's way, and he was instantly on the phone to 'my dearest old friend' and said: *Ralphie, be an angel and think a minute, there's a friend. Should I go to Hollywood and play Heathcliff in Wuthering Heights?* The director, William Wyler, had travelled to London, according to Olivier, *to goose me into it.* Richardson said: 'Yes. Bit of fame. Good.' So he did.

A box-office triumph. Olivier and Merle Oberon in *Wuthering Heights*

He learned a lot about film from Wyler, though he found Wyler's methods irritating after the thoughtful politeness of Coward and Gielgud. *How do you want it?* he once asked Wyler in despair after a dozen takes of a single line of dialogue. *I've done it calm, I've shouted, I've done it angry, sad, standing up, sitting down, fast, slow – how do you want me to do it?* And Wyler said: 'Better.' Olivier still, like most British actors, faintly despised film, a medium in which he thought the director had all the fun, for *the sum total of the actor's work in a picture depends entirely on the arbitrary manner in which the director puts together his mosaic.* He wanted to be the boss, and was not yet distinguished enough. But he looked marvellous, a perfect tragic romantic lead.

He got on badly with his co-star Merle Oberon, partly because he coveted her part for Vivien, and Oberon never forgave him. During the filming, he heard of his father's sudden death of a stroke, in retirement in Sussex at the age of 69.

Vivien, too, was on her way to the USA – in her case, in search of the part for which she is still remembered, that of Scarlett O'Hara in *Gone with the Wind.* Olivier, on his own account, was fiercely ambitious for Vivien and greased some wheels for her; and no doubt he did, but director David Selznick was clear as soon as he met her that this was his Scarlett. While she made the film, Olivier got himself a part in a successful Broadway comedy, partly so that he could continue to be in the USA, seeing Vivien.

Their affair was still, theoretically, a secret, and Olivier's visits to her home had to be made in great secrecy. If they got into the newspapers, Selznick might invoke the clause in her contract which enabled him to fire her for 'moral turpitude.' And in any case, though Olivier was still utterly in love with her, her voracious sexual demands were beginning to exhaust him. She could not wait to be with him, partly for the sex – 'we fucked and we fucked and we fucked and we fucked' was her account of one weekend to a fellow actor – and partly because she did not much enjoy being with the cast of *Gone with the Wind.* Clark Gable's whisky breath irritated her, and so did his false teeth – he had had all his teeth removed and false ones substituted in order to achieve the famous film-star look.

And that is how they came to be in the USA on 3 September 1939. Douglas Fairbanks Junior had taken a yacht for a day, so, just off the island of Catalina, near the California coast, they heard Prime Minister Neville Chamberlain on the radio announcing that Britain was now at war with Germany. They reacted by getting maudlin drunk, and Olivier raced around between the other yachts in a speedboat, shouting 'You are finished, all of you, you are relics, that's what you are.' There was no immediate call for young men like Olivier to return to defend the homeland, and in fact the British ambassador encouraged them to stay to help counter pro-German propaganda in the USA.

Not, it has to be said, that the coming of war seems to have inhibited Laurence and Vivien's ambitious enjoyment of the here and now. He did two more films, *Rebecca* and *Pride and Prejudice*, and then he and Vivien, now newly married, embarked almost at once on *Romeo and Juliet* for the American stage, with Olivier directing as well as playing Romeo.

Olivier and Joan Fontaine in Alfred Hitchcock's adaptation of *Rebecca*

Part of the idea was to make some serious money quickly, and they put all their savings from the films – $96,000, a huge sum in those days – into it.

This was to be a very different Romeo from the 1935 one – a young, uninteresting boy at the start of the play, whose character is shaped by his love for Juliet. As director, he supervised every aspect of the production himself with care and precision – a huge strain when he was still completing a film. He exhausted himself, and was not able to give of his best by the time the play opened.

It opened in San Francisco, where notices were poor; continued to Chicago, where they were lukewarm; and arrived in New York to a merciless critical battering which had queues forming outside the theatre before the second night, full of people who had booked their seats and wanted their money back. They cut back the proposed nine-week run but still had to play for four weeks through a hot New York summer, with thin audiences which were often inclined to laugh at the most dramatic moments. Laurence Olivier and Vivien Leigh would be on stage, miserable. He was thinking – as he confessed later: *Here am I, in uttermost misery, sweating, flinging myself painfully around, tearing my soul to bits, and being paid with shrieks of mocking laughter, and this pleasure is costing me at least a thousand dollars this afternoon.* They lost all the money they had made from *Gone with the Wind* and Olivier's last three films. And almost no one asked them out to supper in New York, for failure is considered contagious. Laurence Olivier did not look as though he was going to have a good war.

The war and the Old Vic

The USA did not enter the Second World War until 1941, when its hand was forced by the Japanese attack on Pearl Harbor. President Franklin Roosevelt was personally strongly anti-Nazi and committed to do what he could to help the Allied cause, but a majority of his fellow countrymen wanted to have nothing to do with European entanglements. Most Americans believed that getting involved in the First World War, bringing the USA for the first time into European quarrels, had been a mistake – a mistake they were not about to repeat in 1939. Even worse, those who cared about the outcome in Europe were not all on Britain's side. There was a strong pro-German element.

So an English actor, however eminent, who found himself beached in New York in 1939, was not likely to be treated as some sort of heroic exile. And an English actor who was being politely shunned by New York society for a universally derided Shakespeare production could start to feel distinctly unwelcome. It was time for Laurence Olivier and Vivien Leigh to go home.

But this was easier said than done, even for someone who now had Olivier's impressive range of contacts, and could ring his friend Duff Cooper, Minister of Information, from the other side of the Atlantic. Ordinary mortals could not make transatlantic calls at all, but Olivier could get through direct to Cooper's office without difficulty. He asked what use he could be to the war effort, and may have been disappointed with the response. Cooper said that conscription did not apply to men over 31 (Olivier was 33) and the actor might be more use in the USA than in Britain.

But Cooper may have helped behind the scenes after all, for a few days later Olivier had a call from Alexander Korda, who wanted to make a film about Lord Nelson and his mistress Lady Hamilton, partly as a money-spinner, and partly to aid British morale and mobilise US opinion behind the war effort. Korda had promised the new Prime Minister Winston Churchill that it would be propaganda for the war effort, focusing in the brave and romantic Lord Nelson; and since he wanted Larry and Vivien for the two leads, it would also repair the large hole in their finances caused by *Romeo and Juliet*.

The resulting film was a triumph for Vivien and rather less of a triumph for her husband, who was required to be little more than a cardboard-cutout English hero, saying Churchillian things

Olivier and Vivien Leigh in *That Hamilton Woman*

like: 'I would not for the sake of any peace, however fortunate, consent to sacrifice one jot of England's honour.' Korda placed her name before his on the credits. Olivier was getting visibly tired of being outshone in films by his leading ladies, from Merle Oberon to Vivien Leigh, and especially those he was married to. But in London Winston Churchill watched the film several times and played it to visiting dignitaries.

Six weeks' filming restored the couple's finances so that they could live in the manner to which they had become accustomed, and, their children safe in the USA and their reputations restored,

The gilded couple on their return to London in 1941

Mr and Mrs Olivier were free to return to a hero's welcome in Britain. They arrived in London in January 1941, having by good luck missed the Blitz, which flattened much of the city, though fortunately not their Chelsea home. There Olivier used his contacts to get into the Fleet Air Arm. During his weeks of training, Vivien, already showing a level of possessiveness that should have alerted her new husband to trouble ahead, insisted on renting a home nearby, though he begged her not to, feeling he needed some space.

After the training Vivien could only visit him at weekends, for she was rehearsing for a new production of Shaw's *The Doctor's Dilemma*. Olivier joined his old friend Ralph Richardson near Winchester. He bought a motorcycle, the better to escape to pubs with Ralphie, who already had one.

Olivier had learned to fly in the USA, but was never very good at it. Neither was Richardson, and they both caused a lot of expensive damage until their commanding officer grounded them. They got hideously drunk, were ejected from a Winchester theatre for trying to join the cast on stage, and were eventually found a new job: repacking parachutes for the trainees. The Fleet Air Arm started to think of these celebrated actors as something of a liability, while Olivier at least was finding his lack of flying success very wounding to his ego, and longing to be back in the theatre – a longing which became acute as he watched his new wife's success in *The Doctor's Dilemma*. He was in what he had once called the real world, and he pined for the world he had left.

So when the chance of doing a film of *Henry V* came up, he was delighted, and his military superiors were equally delighted to give him leave, for they wanted to hold onto the planes he had not already damaged.

Funded by film mogul J Arthur Rank, it was to be an overtly propaganda film, in which Olivier was to reprise his stage performance as the embodiment of English courage. It was also, as it turned out, the project which made Laurence Olivier, not just another front-rank actor along with his friends Richardson, Gielgud and others, but the moment when he leapfrogged all these great contemporaries. The reason for this was that he also directed the film; and that was, or at least looked like, an accident.

This is how it happened. He was finicky about the choice of director, hesitating before agreeing to any name that was offered to him and, though no one knew why, refusing to accept Carol Reed. At last an exasperated Rank said that, if he was going to be difficult, perhaps he ought to undertake the job himself. Perhaps he did not mean to be taken literally, but Olivier agreed, very quickly. For the first time he was going to control the finished film. It was what he had pined for all that time in Hollywood, when he chafed under the tutelage of the likes of William Wyler.

He had ensured that *Henry V* would make or break him. It made him. It was, by any standards, an extraordinary achievement. It opens with a careful and loving recreation of Elizabethan London, and the first scenes are staged in a recreation of Shakespeare's Globe Theatre. Olivier took the huge risk of making most of the film overtly stagey. Before Henry V's first entrance we catch him behind the scenes, coughing to clear his throat, then mentally getting in character before striding onto the stage: an Elizabethan actor preparing. Some early scenes were performed as farce in the gallery above the stage. Even when the action moves away from the Globe, the sets are still stagey, painted ones – the chorus says two lines taken from elsewhere in the play: 'Still be kind/ And eke out our performance with your mind.'

The only realistic scene is the Battle of Agincourt itself, a model for the real war then raging. It was the most realistic battle scene ever filmed up to that time.

The battle was shot in Ireland – partly because the scenery in Lord Powerscourt's Enniskery estate looked right, partly to be safe from air raids, and partly to avoid paying the extras the Equity minimum rate. Olivier himself chose the horsemen to double for his principal actors. He had his fingers in every aspect of production, and did every stunt, never asking anyone to do anything he would not do himself. Throughout his career Laurence Olivier never spared his own body, doing things for performance that he would have dreaded if asked to do them for any other purpose, and he often hurt himself.

Being in command of an 'army' of 700 people inspired him and brought out his leadership qualities. He performed the final duel with the Constable of France himself, but had an extra to stand in for Leo Genn, who played the Constable. (The duel is not in Shakespeare's script but made a splendid heroic denouement to the battle.) He sprained an ankle showing his Irish extras how to drop 20 feet from a tree to attack passing horsemen, and a falling camera dislocated his shoulder and tore open his lip. He had demanded that a rider should charge straight at the camera, assuming the horse would turn away at the last moment. His lip bore the scar to the end of his life.

Olivier in *Henry V*

Henry V is that much more effective as a war film because it does not idealise war, and that much more effective as a Shakespeare production because Olivier did not hesitate to change and re-order the playwright's work, taking out speeches he did not want and bringing in some speeches from an earlier play. But it emphasises its Englishness (rather than its Britishness) at every opportunity: the flag of St George is waved reverently, the French town of Calais in pronounced Callace and the son of the French king, the Dauphin, is pronounced Dorfin. And Henry is not presented as simply a youthful hero, but as a determined and sometimes cynical statesman who hardly bothers to hide from Katherine that he is wooing her, not out of love, but out of statesmanship.

Olivier is the one and only star. Felix Aylmer makes a comic, bumbling Archbishop of Canterbury, Leo Genn a cynical Constable of France, and there is a splendid short anti-war speech from a young actor playing the boy, George Cole. Renee Asherson made a clever, thoughtful Princess Katherine of France – the part Olivier had wanted for Vivien. But Vivien was still under contract to David Selznick as part of the *Gone with the Wind* deal, and Selznick refused to allow her to appear, saying it was too small a part and would lessen the value of his investment.

Shakespeare, Oliver reflected later, *in a way wrote for the films. His splitting up of the action into a multitude of small scenes is almost an anticipation of film technique, and more than one of his plays seems to chafe against the cramping restrictions of the stage.*

Meanwhile in the real world, Allied forces landed on the Normandy beaches in June 1944, and the German lines were slowly pushed back. The tide of war had changed, and Allied leaders felt confident of ultimate victory, so much so that Lord Beveridge was already drawing up plans for a kinder, fairer post war Britain in which the 'five giants' – Want, Ignorance, Disease, Squalor and Idleness – would have been slain.

The next month *Henry V* was ready – in a sense, too late, for it depicted English forces fighting overwhelming odds. But it caught a mood, and quickly recouped the £475,708 it cost, becoming the most successful as well as the most expensive British film ever made.

And while he was finishing the film, came the perfect invitation. Would he be co-director with Ralph Richardson and John

Burrell of the revived Old Vic company? The company had not played much since a bomb caved in the theatre's roof in 1941. (Bombs destroyed three London theatres, and the Old Vic was one of another three which were seriously damaged.) However, the governors wanted to revive the Old Vic company, playing at another theatre, and hired the Albery Theatre for the purpose. The Admiralty agreed that the two actors need not return to military service: perhaps with a sigh of relief, and at any rate, as Olivier put it, with an alacrity that seemed almost hurtful.

John Burrell, ten years younger than the other two, was a pivotal figure. Polio in his childhood had left him dependent on crutches and with one leg in irons, but he was an ambitious and imaginative theatre director with fierce ambition and a will of steel.

The first three productions were swiftly decided: Ibsen's *Peer Gynt* with Richardson in the title role, then Olivier and Richardson together in Bernard Shaw's *Arms and the Man* with Burrell directing, and Olivier starring in *Richard III*. They started rehearsing in June 1944 just as the flying bombs started hitting London, and rehearsals were frequently interrupted as the company ducked under tables.

He was terrified of Richard III, and, in his worst moments of panic, was convinced that Richardson had set him up with the part in order to destroy him. But it was a triumph. From the first moment, as he limped towards the audience – 'Now is the winter of our discontent/ Made glorious summer by this sun of York' – he dominated the theatre as never before.

He found the character, as he always said an actor should find a character, from the outside – creating the external details and then working inwards. Richard began with the hump, the limp, the sharp nose and the makeup. The actor who tries to do it the other way, working outwards from himself, finds only himself, he said.

After the play had been running a few days, a long, slender package was delivered at the theatre. It contained the sword worn by Edmund Kean when he played Richard III in 1814. On its blade was a new inscription: 'This sword, given him by his mother Kate Terry Gielgud, 1938, is given to Laurence Olivier by his friend John Gielgud in appreciation of his performance of Richard III at the New Theatre, 1944.'

Vivien was pregnant. She ignored Olivier's plea not to work and agreed to film *Caesar and Cleopatra*, and she fell badly on the set, and miscarried. She had a daughter by her first marriage, but she desperately wanted to be the mother of Laurence Olivier's child, a happiness that was denied to her. By then Olivier's and Jill Esmond's son Tarquin Olivier was back in England, having been introduced at the age of eight to his father, whom he did not remember, though he knew what he looked like because he had seen *Henry V*, and he had told all his friends he was Laurence Olivier's son. Tarquin recalls with shame that he was glad when he heard Vivien Leigh had miscarried. He says: 'Larry and Vivien's love was founded on the unhappiness of others – their spouses and their children – and they felt guilty about that.'

But Leigh and Olivier were professionals first. Olivier went on stage that night, and Vivien returned to the film set as soon as she was able. Acting was, even more than before, their life. They bought a grand thirteenth-century 22-room abbot's lodge in Buckinghamshire, called Notley Abbey, with 70 acres and a care-taker's cottage. Olivier directed his wife in Thornton Wilder's *The Skin of Our Teeth*. David Selznick again tried to stop her – he still had her under contract – but her lawyers pointed out that Selznick had no London film studio and could suffer no loss if she appeared on stage in London. Then, soon after the German surrender in 1945, the Old Vic company left for an eight-week European tour, while Vivien stayed in London performing *The Skin of Our Teeth*.

On tour, some of the company, including Sybil Thorndike, took the opportunity to visit the recently liberated camp of

Olivier and his son Tarquin meet backstage after a West End performance

Belsen. Olivier, professional to the point of excluding the real world lest it cloud his theatrical judgement, refused, waving off his colleagues with the words: 'Don't forget the matinee, mind.'

It was on that tour that the simmering professional rivalry between Olivier and Ralph Richardson boiled over into an ugly and dangerous scene.

Richardson, even more than Olivier, had been brought up in genteel poverty. His mother left his father, taking four-year-old Ralph with her, and the two of them lived on the small sums that his father, a teacher and would-be painter, was able to send them. His two older brothers stayed with his father. He went to a series of Catholic schools, where he disliked the intolerance but was captivated by the ceremonial. He never thought of acting until, at the age of 18, he chanced to see *Hamlet* at the Theatre Royal, Brighton. He was tall, burly, strong, with a face that forever debarred him from matinee idol status.

The Richardsons were a rather dangerous lot. One of his brothers shot dead a fellow soldier in France during the First World War because he didn't like something the man was saying. He was spared execution and released from prison because his engineering skills were needed, but it was, as Ralph Richardson said when telling the story, 'a bit hard on the other chap.' Ralph himself, early in his theatrical career, punched his first manager when he was refused his promised pay, and years later, as an eminent actor, knocked down his friend Alec Guinness just because he was in a filthy mood. He had a lifelong addition to fast motorcycles, and was still terrorising the streets of London in his eighties.

Richardson was also, at this time, recovering slowly and painfully from a dreadful tragedy. His wife, a promising actress called Muriel Hewitt, was caught in the epidemic of the disease encephalitis lethargica in 1927. Those who did not die at once lost their faculties and faded slowly into sleepy lethargy until eventually they did die. After dispiriting years handled by both of them with courage and dignity, she died in 1942, at the age of 35. Two years later he married the actress who had been his companion in the last years of his wife's illness, Meriel Forbes, always known as Mu.

Richardson envied Olivier his glamour and box-office appeal. Olivier envied Richardson his apparently effortless talent and stage presence, for Olivier never for one moment stopped wanting, desperately, to be, indisputably, the best. They quarrelled about who was doing better, who was getting better notices. 'I hate him' Richardson once said 'until I see him. Then he has more magnetism than anyone I've ever met.' A fellow actor, Harry Andrews, saw at the Old Vic, when they took their solo bows at the end of a production, that the applause was massive for Olivier and started to die a little when Richardson came on. But one night Richardson's applause was much louder than Olivier's. Olivier said: 'Hell, the bastard, why the hell has he done that to me?' 'And he meant it' said Andrews.

How deep and bitter the rivalry went, no one realised, not even the two of them, until one terrible night it came to the boil in Paris. The city had not long been liberated, and many Parisians were still starving – there was not enough to eat in the city. They were also sorting out themselves and their politicians: who had collaborated, who had been with the Resistance, who should live and who should die. Into that maelstrom came a great English theatre company, and what was on their minds was who should open: Richardson with *Peer Gynt*, or Olivier with *Richard III*. Olivier knew that the first one would be the big one so far as the critics were concerned, so he told Richardson that, as *Peer Gynt* had opened first in London, *Richard III* must open first in Paris. Richardson felt forced, with great reluctance, to agree.

Richard III opened, a massive success, and that night Olivier went back to his hotel bedroom. Richardson must have gone out and tried to soothe his fury and jealousy with a massive quantity of alcohol; for at last he stormed into Olivier's room, grabbed him, and picked him up – he was, it turned out, much physically stronger than his rival, despite Olivier's fanatical fitness regime designed to ensure that he could do all the stage stunts he wanted.

Richardson carried the struggling Olivier to the balcony and held him over it, 60 feet above the Paris street. Olivier held himself still, sure that if he struggled his furious rival would let him fall, and that would be the end of him. *Ralph* he said *I think we'll all look very silly in the morning.* Still Richardson held him. *Why don't you pull me back? I'm beginning to feel really nervous.*

Ralph Richardson

After a long pause, very slowly, Richardson did pull him back, and trudged off to his own room.

Over breakfast, Olivier said: *Ralph, that was rather a near one, wasn't it?*

'Yes' replied Richardson. 'We were both very foolish. It was a double fault.' Olivier's reflections on it seem oddly ethereal, as though it happened in a play: *Whatever else, (Ralph) was a great man. They were golden days, and we were the golden boys, blessed with God's sunshine.*

And perhaps he understood that he had used his instinctive political talents too ruthlessly against a man who did not possess them; for when the company went back to London, he suggested that Richardson should open as Falstaff. This turned out to be one of Richardson's greatest triumphs, and he never ceased to be grateful to Olivier for giving him the inspiration and encouragement to undertake it. Olivier himself played Shallow, filling the part with farcical moments.

While they were abroad, *The Skin of Our Teeth* closed and Vivien went down with tuberculosis. At Notley Abbey, she recuperated while he prepared for the next Old Vic season, which offered some of his most legendary performances. As Oedipus in the W B Yeats translation of *Oedipus Rex*, he emitted cries of anguish that chilled the audience, inspired by something he had read about ermine trappers, who, he found, spread salt on the ice. The animals tried to lick off the salt and their tongues froze to the ice, so that they wailed in agony as the trappers came to club them to death.

Weekends, at Notley, were full of Vivien's parties, always splendid, always carefully and lovingly arranged, always with a dozen or so guests; for Vivien was being forced, much against her will, to rest, and was putting her restless energy into their social life. For her husband, it all made for an exhausting winter. In the spring of 1946 the Old Vic company departed for a six-week American tour, and Vivien, still not entirely well, went along for the ride.

So by the summer of that year, Laurence Olivier was in a state of complete exhaustion, driving himself to complete the massive schedule he had set for himself and keep up with Vivien as well. Audiences did not know – he was ever the professional, ever the trouper, and he was the toast of New York, always drawing the longest applause at the end of every performance. But those he worked with knew. They saw him tense and haggard, they were at the sharp end of his temper, they woke him sometimes between scenes from a short nap backstage.

To add to Olivier's troubles, costs in New York were higher than they had expected. They stayed at an expensive hotel – *it would have been misunderstood if we had sought somewhere more economical* explained Olivier. But the actors accepted tiny salaries, and even the two stars, Olivier and Richardson, took what Olivier describes as *a modest salary by the general standards of leading players in New York*. He rescued his personal finances (of course he was by now a rich man, though no more likely to stop worrying about money than his late father) with a cunning offer to Victor Records. He suggested they pay him to make records of excerpts from *Henry V*, with William Walton (who composed the music for the film) conducting the London Philharmonic. But – said Olivier – he was exhausted right now. Could he please do the work when he was back in London, but have the money straight away? They agreed.

Back in London, rested, Olivier and Richardson planned the next season. They did it with all the convoluted jealousy which characterised their relationship. In a meeting with their co-director John Burrell, Richardson said he wanted to play Cyrano de Bergerac. Olivier was furious because it was a part he coveted, and he thought Richardson knew this. So he named for himself the one part he thought his rival and colleague wanted to play one day: King Lear. After the meeting they went to the Garrick pub, opposite the Garrick Theatre, ordered half pints, and Olivier said, no doubt rather smugly: 'Well, so you want to swap?' And Richardson beat him at his own game. 'Oh, no, no' he said, decisively. So Olivier played Lear for the first time. Noel Coward saw him do it, and wrote in his diary: 'He is a superb actor and I suspect the greatest I shall ever see.' But not everyone thought the same. The critic James Agate thought it inferior to Donald Wolfit's recent Lear, which must have annoyed Olivier, for Wolfit was not an actor he admired. Alec Guinness, who played the Fool, thought Olivier technically brilliant but shallow, and thought he undermined other actors to boost his own status. The performance everyone acclaimed was Alec Guinness's Fool.

A weekend at Notley Abbey with Richardson turned into another comic disaster. Richardson was terrified of disgracing himself again – he knew the Oliviers thought twice about inviting him after his performance with the fireworks nearly a decade earlier. He went about carefully, even going tamely on a tour of the house with Olivier while their wives stayed talking downstairs. And on that tour, somehow, he managed to fall through a ceiling, or at least put his foot through it (versions of the story differ), creating a dreadful mess. Vivien was not pleased.

The mutual jealousy between the two actors flared up again when the new year honours list came out in 1947. Richardson became Sir Ralph. *I should have been the fucking knight* said Olivier, backstage at the Old Vic. *I've done every bit as much as he has . . . – and there was a little film called Henry V.* Sir Stafford Cripps, who that year became Chancellor of the Exchequer and was close to Prime Minister Clement Attlee, explained to one of Olivier's friends: 'Unfortunately the chap has only been divorced three years.' He was corrected: it was seven years. But through the jealousy there was a friendship that sustained their partnership. As Richardson's biographer Garry O'Connor puts it: 'Neither was easily offended by the other; neither gave away the other's confidences . . . One cannot talk to Richardson about Olivier without fealing this fundamental respect . . .'

That winter was the coldest on record, when the elements combined with the emerging Cold War to smother the optimism and idealism of 1945 under a frozen shroud. The food minister John Strachey was being pilloried for not feeding the nation and the coal minister Emanuel Shinwell was being pilloried for not keeping it warm – 'Starve with Strachey and shiver with Shinwell' people were saying, bitterly. At the Old Vic, they shivered as they rehearsed and the reason was explained to Ralph Richardson when he was shown a newspaper story about Shinwell. He looked up and said: 'Shinwell. Bad notices.'

Yet in a government led by the quiet, unflamboyant Clement Attlee, the stiff, austere Stafford Cripps – 'austerity Cripps' as he would soon be known – still found time to hear Laurence Olivier's resentment about Ralph Richardson's knighthood.

The food minister John Strachey was being pilloried for not feeding the nation and the coal minister Emanuel Shinwell was being pilloried for not keeping it warm – 'Starve with Strachey and shiver with Shinwell' people were saying, bitterly.

Olivier's own knighthood came a few months later, and it mattered to him very much indeed. He then made a great show of asking Noel Coward's permission before accepting, since Coward would doubtless have had a knighthood if he had not been a homosexual.

Fortunately, Coward was not so foolish as to ask him to turn it down. Olivier once said his knighthood was *sacred* to him.

Then came the second of the great Shakespeare films which are, as much as anything, what Laurence Olivier will be remembered for. His Old Vic schedule gave him time to make the occasional film. His 1947 *Hamlet* is not quite the towering achievement that his *Henry V* is, but it is a powerful, brooding film, set in a bleak castle hemmed in by huge waves from the sea and dark, glowering clouds. It was deliberately shot in black and white for the atmosphere.

At the age of 40, it was convenient for him to embrace the tradition he had found so frustrating in his Birmingham Rep days, of the great but middle-aged actor-manager playing the youthful Hamlet. *It was ancient custom* he wrote in his memoirs *for the most ancient actor-managers to play Hamlet; I am sure Irving was in his sixties before finishing with the part.* Hamlet's mother Gertrude was played by an actress 13 years younger than himself, Eileen Herlie. Hamlet's lover Ophelia was a big break for an actress aged just 18, Jean Simmons, and it justly made her a star. Vivien wanted the part, and Olivier had the nerve to tell her she was too old at 33. Vivien decided (wrongly) that Simmons must be having an affair with her husband, and took to descending on the set.

The interpretation, as usual with Olivier, is rammed home, so that the most inattentive audience could not fail to perceive it.

Oliver directs a damp and probably cold Jean Simmons in *Hamlet*

The play is, according to a voice dark with meaning over the credits 'the tragedy of a man who could not make up his mind.' His
Hamlet is fey, distracted, obsessed by his inner turmoil, frozen
into inaction. He is relaxed only at the moments when he thinks
he has found a way to avoid doing anything decisive – when he is
with the actors, and thinks they are going to solve the problem for
him: 'The play's the thing/ Wherein I'll catch the conscience of
the king.' The Oedipus theme he had taken in 1937 from
Professor Jones was spelled out unmistakably right at the start,
when Gertrude kisses an unresponsive Hamlet long and passion-
ately on the lips, only stopping when she is pulled away by her
husband. The famous 'To be or not to be' speech, in which Hamlet
contemplates suicide, takes place on a rampart with occasional
shots at the rocks beneath, at which great waves unremittingly
fling themselves.

Olivier may have been an actor; but he was also a man of action. He did not agonise; he got on with it. That is where he and Hamlet parted company. He makes the king, Claudius, turn aside to say with special meaning the lines that made Olivier the director he was: 'We should do what we would do when we would.' And as he had done with *Henry V*, only more so, he did not hesitate to do whatever he thought proper to Shakespeare's text, cutting almost half of it, getting rid of whole sub-plots and much-loved characters like Rosencrantz and Guildenstern, modernising the language.

Olivier never missed an opportunity for spectacle or for farce. Stanley Holloway made a delightful cameo appearance as the gravedigger, using for Shakespeare's dialogue much the same voice as he used for his famous Yorkshire monologues like *Albert and the Lion*. The pompous messenger, gloriously hammed, falls backwards down the steps as he bows his way from Hamlet's presence. And Olivier insisted on doing a dangerous climactic jump from a 15-foot high balcony onto Claudius in the last scene.

Back at the Old Vic company, the seeds of a project of long term significance were being sewn. Olivier and Richardson believed that the Old Vic company, successful though it was, could not last unless it had its own theatre; and the Old Vic itself was still unusable. Meanwhile a committee to establish a National Theatre was working under the chairmanship of Oliver Lyttelton, a leading Conservative politician (the Conservatives were in opposition, Labour having won the 1945 election, and Labour leader Clement Attlee was Prime Minister.) 'It'll be the end of us' Richardson told him. 'It'll be of government interest now, with some appointed intendant swell at the top, not our sweet old friendly governors eating out of our hands and doing as we tell them. They're not going to stand for a couple of actors bossing the place around any more. We shall be out, old cockie. But I still think we may have done the right thing.'

The tragedy of Vivien Leigh

By the end of 1947 Laurence Olivier felt he had everything he could possibly want. He was rich. He was starting to be acknowledged as the greatest actor of his generation, edging ahead of his old rivals Ralph Richardson and John Gielgud. He had his cherished knighthood, and an almost equally cherished Rolls Royce. He lived in a beautiful home with the woman he loved. Always happiest at work, he was working constantly. An instinctive conservative, he was probably not over the moon about austere, Labour-run Britain – he voted Conservative in 1945 – but he did not spend much of his time thinking about such things. He was a happy man.

And then it started to fall apart. The rot started when the Old Vic company toured Australia and New Zealand for ten months at the request of the British Council.

Olivier led the tour, while Richardson went to Hollywood. The actor Cedric Hardwicke was left in charge of the company's London productions, and the 30-year-old Alec Guinness was trying to fill Olivier's shoes in London. Vivien Leigh joined the

Olivier and Vivien Leigh in *School for Scandal*

tour, the first time she had worked in the company. They took Sheridan's *The School for Scandal*, Thornton Wilder's *The Skin of Our Teeth*, and Shakespeare's *Richard III*.

On this tour, Olivier grew to dread playing Richard III, especially on matinee days when he had to perform it twice. During one performance, he tore a cartilage in his right knee, which had been weakened from the limp he used as Richard, so that he had to use a crutch for the part in future.

Soon after that, a letter arrived from the Old Vic, saying that he, Richardson and Burrell were fired. Richardson in Hollywood received the same letter, and so did Burrell in London.

It was just what Richardson had prophesied, only faster and more brutal. Now that the Old Vic company was associated with the National Theatre project, the board did not want it run by two famous theatrical knights with their own following. Board members would rather have an administrator who would take their instructions. They used as an excuse the fact that the London company was not quite as good as it had been, with so many of its leading players in Australia and Richardson in America. Garry O'Connor's biography of Ralph Richardson offers a glimpse of the small-minded jealousy which brought about the decision.

'At first a whispering campaign began, the detractors of the company exaggerating its decline . . . These same detractors would gloat over items which lauded "Sir Laurence Olivier's Old Vic company" on the Australian tour; "Whose Old Vic?" they would ask in superior fashion.' The letter, from the chairman, Lord Esher, was a four-page document saying that the company 'cannot be administered by men, however able, who have other calls upon their time and talent.'

And soon after that came another blow to Olivier. He wrote: *Somehow, somewhere on this tour I knew that Vivien was lost to me.* But as so often in his memoirs, this suggests it was all the other person's fault, and that was not true at all. It would be truer to say they were lost to each other.

She flirted outrageously with young men in the company, largely to gain Olivier's attention, and at this stage it seems to have gone no further than that. She took no pleasure from the adulation accorded her, believing she was just seen as an Olivier appendage. And it was in Australia that they met the man who was eventually to claim her affection, a promising young Australian actor whom Olivier immediately put under contract, called Peter Finch.

At first a whispering campaign began, the detractors of the company exaggerating its decline . . . These same detractors would gloat over items which lauded "Sir Laurence Olivier's Old Vic company" on the Australian tour; "Whose Old Vic?" they would ask in superior fashion.

Ralph Richardson, An Actor's Life by Garry O'Connor.

In Australia, Olivier became almost lordly. Henry V, the knighthood, the deference of Australians to the great actor, the way they mobbed him for his autograph and made him reply to the loyal toast on every conceivable occasion so that he almost felt as though he were representing the King, being asked to inspect troops and take salutes – it all seemed to give him an air of grandeur. *When a man is British* he typically told a Melbourne gathering *he is constantly finding himself proud of being so . . . Britain is not finished.*

In New Zealand he was a curiosity. The old gibe about New Zealand – 'I went there once, but it was Monday and the place was shut' – is outdated now, but in those days there was something to be said for it. Pubs were open for just half an hour at the end of the working day, which caused what New Zealanders called the 'six o'clock swill' when men charged into the pub and forced down as much beer as they could before they were thrown out. Restaurants closed at nine. The theatre was almost unknown.

They drew packed houses, but the company was so exhausted

that they took little pleasure from it. The slow disintegration of the Oliviers' marriage became painfully apparent to the rest of their company. One night, Vivien could not find the red shoes she needed for Lady Teazle in *The School for Scandal*, and Olivier told her to put on any shoes available. She said it was the red shoes or nothing, he slapped her face and said *Get up on that stage, you little bitch*, she hit him back, saying 'Don't you dare hit me, you bastard' – and then, like the professional she was, she dried her tears, assumed her character, and moments later walked on stage wearing modern black shoes beneath her floor-length gown.

The Oliviers' coffers showed a hefty profit from the tour, and the company got a bonus – though a rather small one, just £60 each. Like his father, Olivier was always careful with money, however much he had of it.

Neither Olivier nor Richardson allowed the bureaucratic manoeuvring that took the Old Vic away from them to poison their lives. They were never seen to feed the press fury when the news leaked. Olivier had for some time maintained a shadow company called Laurence Olivier Productions, so now he activated it, and it became the vehicle for his London productions.

Many of these featured his new protégé, Peter Finch. Finch's parents had abandoned him in Australia when they left for England, leaving him with a need for security and a yearning to know his parents. Sexually, he was – as one commentator put it – hyperactive. Olivier saw him as a great talent and as a younger version of himself; and some people at the time thought they saw in the bisexual Olivier a sexual longing for the young Finch.

Whether Olivier felt that or not, there is no doubt his wife did. In 1949 she told Olivier she was no longer in love with him. But she felt she needed him, as friend, protector, adviser – the same sort of role she had once allotted to her first husband, Leigh Holman.

Neither of the Oliviers felt like going through the scandal of another divorce. But sexually, they were bored with each other.

She wanted far more sex than he did – she complained rather cuttingly about it, and he reacted by removing himself yet further from her. She also suspected his sexual ambivalence, the amount of time he seemed to want to spend with attractive young men, often either Peter Finch or another younger man to whom he was becoming very close, the American comedian Danny Kaye. The intimacy with Vivien was disappearing along with the sex, and their conversations were increasingly confined to work. *We never converse*, Olivier confided to a friend. *We only confer.*

The Olivier 'brand' combined his glamour with hers, but her career had been somewhat subordinated to his, and she had not had a big success since *Gone With the Wind*. Now, however, there was a chance of another – she was to play, under Olivier's direction, the massive, terrifying part of Blanche Du Bois in Tennessee Williams' *A Streetcar Named Desire*, the play that had made Marlon Brando a Broadway star as the thuggish brother-in-law who exposes Blanche Du Bois' sad lies and pretensions, and rapes her. Du Bois ends the play being taken to a lunatic asylum, saying as she is led out: 'I have always relied on the kindness of strangers.'

He worked her ferociously, and she sought his guidance on every small aspect of her performance. She was terrified of the part: frightened of getting it wrong, frightened too, perhaps, of letting Blanche Du Bois' madness become Vivien Leigh's madness. She played it for eight months. No one knows the long

Marlon Brando and Vivien Leigh in *A Streetcar Named Desire* term effect it had on her, but some of her friends say that it took her a year to recover from being Blanche Du Bois. It was, say most of those who saw it, a great performance, and it brought her a second Oscar to add to the one she had won for *Gone with the Wind*.

In 1949 Olivier took a four-year lease on the St James's, a charming small theatre in King Street, just south of Piccadilly, which dated from 1835. They started with Christopher Fry's *Venus Observed*, a verse play which Olivier had commissioned; he directed it and played the lead. Then came two plays showcasing Peter Finch, both of which Olivier directed.

But the Oliviers never managed to make the St James's pay. Post-war London theatre was not an easy place to stage serious drama. There was a large entertainments tax, 10 per cent of gross profits, which made West End shows financially shaky, though the newly-formed Arts Council had the power to cancel the tax for some shows with some cultural credibility – *A Streetcar Named Desire* benefited from this. Repertory theatres were struggling for survival against competition from the infant television, and from radio, which was having the best years of its history, the years when it introduced the world to *The Goons, Hancock's Half Hour, Beyond Our Ken* and *The Archers*.

A war-weary nation seemed inclined to settle for innocuous light comedies. A predominantly wealthy West End audience, shocked at the socialist landslide of 1945, seemed to crave the restoration of what it saw as a proper balance between the classes. They were rewarded in 1948 with William Douglas Home's *The Chiltern Hundreds*, a vacuous comedy which showed an uppity socialist defeated in an election by a Conservative butler. In 1950 the Whitehall farces, led by Brian Rix, replaced the pre-war Aldwych farces – the first was *Reluctant Heroes*. They made their money on a new kind of audience, the coach trade – local clubs or pubs putting together sufficient people to earn a discount at the box office. The same trade sustained

Agatha Christie's *The Mousetrap*, which opened in 1952 and is still running.

Laurence Olivier and Vivien Leigh fed the hunger to have stars people could admire, to help them forget their drab post-war ration-book lives. They were the most famous of several glittering stage partnerships of the time: Michael Denison and Dulcie Grey, John Mills and Mary Hayley Bell, Michael Redgrave and Rachel Kempson, Michael Denison and Dulcie Gray.

This celebrity was part of what kept them together, though they were no longer in love. Olivier's recent knighthood, which he called *sacred* to him, was a factor too – he knew it had been delayed because of his first divorce, and seems to have felt that if he divorced again, he would be made to feel he had been honoured under false pretensions. But principally, their celebrity was what enabled them to subsidise the loss-making St James's with their film work, as well as by occasionally letting out the theatre to other managers. The era of the great actor-manager had drawn to its end before the war, and only Olivier's great prestige and the glamour of the two of them together made it at all viable.

But he was now clear that he wanted to be more and more involved with management. His problems were, first, that he had not yet foreseen the 1950s move towards realism and away from lavish costume dramas (though eventually he was among the first of his generation to see it); and second, that his sort of productions were very expensive, demanding splendid costumes and sets as well as a large troupe of actors, which was increasingly unafford- able at a time of sharply rising costs, when you had to bring in audiences still steeped in wartime austerity.

One of the films that subsidised the St James's was *A Streetcar Named Desire*: Vivien Leigh was asked to repeat her Blanche Du Bois in Hollywood, while her husband made *Carrie* with William Wyler, developing a perfect mid-west accent for the part. In Hollywood they grew further apart. Olivier and Danny Kaye became lovers; and Vivien toured Hollywood hotspots seeking sexual pleasure where she could find it.

Olivier's memoirs make no mention of this affair with Danny Kaye. By implication he denies it, for he talks of the *one man* with whom he could have a sexual relationship, and is clearly referring to Noel Coward. But he did own up to the affair in a private letter to Vivien a decade later – unnecessarily, because she knew about it at the time. By 1950, Vivien Leigh's persistent sexual demands, once so exciting for him, had become a burden. Kaye pursued him, flattered him, corralled both Oliviers into performing vaudeville numbers with him at charity benefits, got himself invited to the places where they would be.

Back in London in February 1951, Laurence and Vivien appeared together at the St James's, alternating Shaw's *Caesar and*

Olivier and Vivien Leigh on stage in *Anthony and Cleopatra*

Cleopatra and Shakespeare's *Anthony and Cleopatra*. It was a brave and clever idea, they put all their extraordinary energy and talent into it, and they were rewarded with a huge success. The theatre-going public loved it and sustained it for 155 performances; and it had wonderful notices from every critic except one.

That one was the new boy in the block, the 24-year-old drama critic of the *Spectator*, Kenneth Tynan. Tynan, looking to make a name for himself, was almost certainly brutally unfair to Vivien Leigh, but his verdict – that she was not up to Olivier, that her performance diminished his, that her reputation was based on her association with him – has coloured how Vivien Leigh has been seen ever since. 'How obsequiously' wrote Tynan, 'Sir Laurence seems to play along with her . . . Blunting his iron precision, levelling away his towering authority, he meets her halfway.' We cannot, sadly, see the truth for ourselves, but we can see Vivien Leigh's film performances, and these suggest that Tynan's colleagues were right and he was wrong. She was a much greater actress than Tynan would have us believe. As for Olivier, what Tynan took to be a deliberately subdued performance was really, according to other commentators, a subtle interpretation of his two characters: Anthony dissatisfied with himself, Caesar weary, lonely, tired, bored even with his own achievements.

Tynan never stopped attacking Leigh's reputation, belittling her, saying she was overrated and threatened Olivier's greatness, and never stopped hero-worshipping Olivier. Put together, his writing about her has a mean and vindictive quality. Yet he was part of the Olivier circle, frequently invited to Notley where Vivien Leigh had to pretend she did not mind. She minded dreadfully. In later years Olivier told Tynan that his reviews had been responsible for at least one of Leigh's nervous breakdowns.

Olivier, characteristically, was overwhelmed one night to know that Winston Churchill was in the audience, and later to dine with him several times shortly before Churchill returned as

Prime Minister in 1951. The great actor was – there's no other word for it – star-struck. But he also turned the relationship to good use. When he and Ralph Richardson received their knighthoods, John Gielgud was passed over, partly because, discreet though he was, his homosexuality was known about in establishment circles. It cannot have been easy to persuade the very old-fashioned Churchill to overlook this; but Olivier succeeded, and Gielgud was knighted in the June 1953 honours list, just hours before the coronation.

Four months later, Establishment figures were demanding that Gielgud should be stripped of it, and horsewhipped in the streets – he was caught importuning, when rather drunk, in a public lavatory in Chelsea. Newspapers and politicians whipped themselves into a frenzy about it, and Gielgud briefly went to pieces and contemplated suicide, but his friends in the theatre sustained him.

This time Laurence Olivier's role seems less loyal. Knowing that Gielgud's career hung in the balance, the powerful theatrical manager Binkie Beaumont, who was staging Gielgud's next show, called a crisis meeting in the flat in Great North Street, Westminster, which Beaumont shared with Gielgud's former lover John Perry. The question was: should Gielgud open in *A Day by the Sea*, as planned, the next week in Liverpool, at the start of its pre-London tour?

Beaumont called in old friends and colleagues – Laurence and Vivien, Glen Byam Shaw and his wife Angela Baddeley, Ralph Richardson and his wife Meriel Forbes. All but one of them said, yes, he must. It would wreck both his career and his confidence if the play was cancelled or he lost his nerve.

The one dissenting voice was that of Laurence Olivier, who thought the production should be delayed for at least three months. Vivien Leigh turned on her husband savagely. He had always been jealous of John, she said, and his view should be discounted.

It was discounted. Gielgud's official biographer Sheridan Morley thinks she was right, and that Olivier 'saw the chance to do his old rival down.' Perhaps this is unfair, but it was certainly a strange kind of solidarity with an old friend. Had Olivier's advice been taken, Gielgud's career would probably have been over; and perhaps his life, too. Gielgud himself always felt he was more Vivien's friend than Larry's; he had much more in common with her, and liked her much better.

John Gielgud travelled to Liverpool, but when his cue came, he was too terrified to go on stage. Sybil Thorndike went into the wings and pulled him out – and the audience gave him a standing ovation. Theatre historian Richard Huggett writes: 'It was a moment never to be forgotten by those who witnessed it, Sybil Thorndike hugging him and smiling with unmistakable defiance at the audience . . . Gielgud, the famous Terry tears visibly running down his cheek, unable to speak. It was a long time before he could stammer out his first line, one of delicious triviality: "Oh dear, I'd forgotten we had all those azaleas," which, at a moment of such cosmic significance, was greeted by a roar of laughter and renewed applause.'

Meanwhile Olivier and Leigh were enjoying the London success of *Caesar and Cleopatra* and *Anthony and Cleopatra*. They then took the two plays to New York, where, when the news of the death of King George VI came through in February 1952, Olivier presided at the New York memorial ceremony, with all the orotund solemnity of the robust monarchist he was.

But in the USA the theatre had to compete with a new medium which was still relatively rare in Britain, television; and audiences were unexpectedly sparse. At the end of one performance, when a small audience produced only thin applause, Olivier whispered to his wife: *Smile at them, baby – smile if it's the last thing you do.* She did, and her smile brought a sudden renewed wave of clapping.

They came back poorer than they had gone. Olivier took on the film of *The Beggars' Opera*, partly to fill the hole in the finances. The set of *The Beggars' Opera* was not a happy place. Peter Brook was director – but Olivier was co-producer, to whom the director was answerable, as well as leading man. As he rightly pointed out in his memoirs, *the position of a director who has less authority than his leading man is a rotten one*, but there is no evidence he made any effort to make it better.

Olivier took singing lessons, and only he and Stanley Holloway did their own singing. The rest, at Brook's insistence, were dubbed. Olivier complained bitterly that this had the effect of making him sound inferior to the rest of the cast – as indeed it did. Perhaps the greatest actor of his generation should have been great enough to realise that some things were better done by others. This was a man who had many times injured himself by insisting that he do his own stunts, and now injured his reputation by insisting on doing his own singing.

During the filming Olivier started an affair with the attractive 22-year-old actress who played Polly Peacham, Dorothy Tutin. Vivien Leigh learned of it, but she seems not to have been quite as devastated as one might have expected, for she had signed for a film called *Elephant Walk*, to be shot in Ceylon, which would make a further contribution to restoring the Olivier finances; and she had chosen her own leading man – Peter Finch. All three of them knew why. In Olivier's occasionally self-serving memoirs there are lyrical passages about the heartbreak she caused him by her affair with Finch, but no mention at all of Dorothy Tutin.

Vivien Leigh had her first nervous breakdown on the set of *Elephant Walk*. There had been indications that all was not well while they were performing in New York. In Ceylon she realised she was just one of a string of affairs in Peter Finch's life. She took to throwing fierce tantrums on the set and screaming speeches from *Streetcar*. Finch ended their affair. An old flame of hers, an actor called John Buckmaster – himself mentally fragile – had taken up residence in her house, apparently suggesting they leap from the rooftop and fly round Beverley Hills. He was ejected by two of her friends.

Olivier was sent for, but the consoling effect of her husband's arrival cannot have been enhanced by the fact that he was accompanied by the solicitous figure of Danny Kaye, with whom he had spent the night during a stopover in New York. Kaye's wife Sylvia was there too: she had long since accepted Kaye's affairs and his sexual ambivalence. Vivien, already being attended by two nurses, told her husband she was in love with Peter Finch.

The film company, generously and rather surprisingly, released her from her contract without penalty, replacing her with Elizabeth Taylor. Vivien was terrified of injections, but Olivier and Kaye held her down while a nurse inserted the syringe, Vivien fighting them furiously all the time, and Olivier took her home. Her parents came to Notley and Olivier asked them if they had any insanity in their family. 'Good God, no' said Vivien's father, and Olivier wanted to say (but stopped himself): 'Well, you have now.' Leaving his wife in hospital to receive, first massive doses of insulin to send her to sleep for three weeks, then several heavy doses of ECT – electric-shock therapy to her brain – he went for a holiday to Italy, not far from a nervous breakdown himself.

Returning, he noted sadly the personality changes inevitable with ECT, a treatment she would have intermittently for the rest of her life. It was, even then, controversial, for no one knew how it worked, but it was clear that it had an adverse effect on the brain which was later dramatised in the gut-wrenching film *One Flew Over the Cuckoo's Nest*. Today it is unlikely she would be prescribed it, and from our standpoint, the decision to force it on her seems monstrous, but at the time Olivier had no doubts, even though *she was no longer the person I had loved. I loved her that much less.* He took her back to Notley Abbey.

There, personal troubles mounted. His older brother Dickie's business folded, leaving him destitute; Olivier made him the manager of the farm at Notley. Thieves stole Vivien's cherished Oscar for *Streetcar* as well as thousands of pounds worth of her furs and jewellery. But she recovered enough to work again.

It was 1953. *This*, wrote Olivier in his great, round, monarchical prose, *was Coronation Year in Britain, and that it should be the last of such for a very long time was everyone's prayer. For now we had a lovely young queen, the first to assume the throne for a hundred years; Elizabeth, Anne, Victoria — they had all ruled over great periods in our country.* Queen Elizabeth II was to inherit, among other things, all the slightly stagy loyalty that Olivier had given to her father George VI and her grandfather George V.

He wanted to perform something special with which he and Vivien could honour the new queen, and Terence Rattigan offered him his new play, *The Sleeping Prince*, set on the eve of the coronation of George V, about the relationship between a European prince and an American chorus girl. It was the only London play he appeared in between 1951 and 1957, and, thin as it was, it did nothing for either of their reputations.

It was time for Olivier to go back to the great Shakespeare parts, to remind the world who he was and what he could do. First there was the film of *Richard III*, which he would direct and produce, and in which he was to play the lead. Then there was the 1955 season in Stratford, at the Shakespeare Memorial Theatre, in which John Gielgud was to direct *Twelfth Night* with Olivier as Malvolio and Vivien Leigh as Viola, and they were also to appear together in *Macbeth* and *Titus Andronicus*.

Richard III, he said later, *is a really difficult play to film — it's involved, often obscure. I felt it absolutely necessary to do more simplification than I've ever done before.* He also, yet again, felt it necessary to do every stunt himself, even waiting until he was sure a battle scene shot was perfect before shouting that he needed help because an arrow had accidentally pierced his leg.

The old friends who had worked with him on his previous Shakespeare films were all there, and so were his friends, rivals and contemporaries Ralph Richardson and John Gielgud, each in a small but effective cameo part. Olivier's Richard was the standard by which future Richards would be judged for the rest of the century. Limping, with padded humpback, deformed hand, long nose, confiding malevolently to the camera, he made the opening soliloquy one of the most famous of all Shakespeare's speeches, and would-be actors imitated his clipped delivery for years: 'Now is the winter of our discontent/ Made glorious summer by this sun of York/ And all the clouds that lowered upon our house/ In the deep bosom of the ocean buried . . .'

Richard III is a really difficult play to film – it's involved, often obscure. I felt it absolutely necessary to do more simplification than I've ever done before.

Laurence Olivier,
Confessions of an Actor.

In Stratford he did enough to put to rest any suggestion that he doused the flame of his talent in order not to outshine his wife. News of the Oliviers' arrival caused the entire season to be sold out well in advance. His Malvolio was a modest triumph, and his Macbeth was a major one. Michael Billington has written: 'He invested the character with a brooding inwardness in the early scenes as if he had been living with bloody thoughts for a long time' and at the end there was 'a heart wrenching despair.' Donald Spoto adds: 'Olivier made Macbeth recognisably human – reluctant, emotionally sallow, and ill.' It was, by general consent, one of the great performances of his career. Eminent critic Harold Hobson called it 'the best Macbeth since Macbeth. I do not believe there is an actor in the world who can come near him.' It is a great loss to us that he was not able to raise the money to film *Macbeth*.

> Olivier was the best Macbeth since Macbeth. I do not believe there is an actor in the world who can come near him.
>
> *Harold Hobson.*

And in Peter Brook's production of *Titus Andronicus* he took on a part which most actors in the past had given up as hopeless. One critic – James Agate – had once complained that, fine physical actor though he was, he could not deliver high tragedy. After *Macbeth* and *Titus Andronicus*, no one ever said that again.

These achievements are all the more remarkable because his personal life was in a bigger mess than ever. Only a great actor, who can escape from himself into the part he is playing, could have done his best work in such miserable circumstances. Not that he was an innocent party; he could hardly complain about Vivien reviving her affair with Peter Finch, having himself, on the set of *Richard III*, found yet another young actress to go to bed with, this time 23-year-old Claire Bloom; and in Stratford he took comfort in the arms of another, Maxine Audley.

Vivien Leigh was, however, utterly indiscreet and seemed not to care how much she humiliated her husband. In Stratford she would invite the company back to their rented house, and in the small hours she would leave Olivier there to go to stay with Finch in his hotel. When they went for weekends at Notley, Finch, and other guests, went too. She no longer had any sexual relationship with Olivier and was obsessed by Finch – who realised he was in deeper than he wanted, but seemed not to know what to do about it. Olivier, to whom the play always came first, would probably have been furious if Finch had walked out on her then: it would have destroyed her performance. 'The Oliviers' noted Noel Coward 'are trapped by public acclaim, scrabbling about in the cold ashes of a physical passion that burnt itself out years ago. Their life together is really hideous.'

Vivien also had to contend with the critics, who compared her unfavourably with her husband – though most without the venom of Kenneth Tynan, who never stopped sneering at her, calling her Lady Macbeth 'competent in its small way.' But the director, John Gielgud – probably in this case a more reliable witness – said simply: 'Both she and Larry were to my mind superb.' The criticisms hurt her badly, and certainly contributed to the sad denouement. By the end of the season she found Olivier's mere presence a torment, and she summoned Finch and went with him to France. Soon afterwards, Finch ended their affair, this time forever.

Neither Olivier nor Leigh behaved particularly well. Olivier arrived at the first Stratford rehearsal with his own interpretations, and in the case of *Twelfth Night*, it was an interpretation he knew his director, John Gielgud, would not like. He played Malvolio for laughs, making him, according to Michael Billington, 'a bumptious arriviste with severe vowel problems.' Gielgud said: 'He insisted on falling backwards off a bench in the garden scene, though I begged him not to do it. He was inclined to be obstinate.'

This was putting it carefully and diplomatically. Gielgud was a great theatre director, though still, in both his own estimation and that of the public, diminished by his conviction for soliciting in 1953, at a time when homosexuality was still a criminal offence – the careers of many distinguished men had come to an abrupt halt when their homosexuality was revealed. He was also a man who spoke in a kind of stream of consciousness, and was therefore very indiscreet. His most famous indiscretion occurred over lunch, when he spoke of someone as being 'an even bigger bore than Eddie Knoblock', then, remembering the name of his lunch companion, adding: 'I don't mean you, the other Eddie Knoblock.' At a dinner party he called someone's performance 'as dreadful as poor, dear Athene on a very bad night,' then, noticing Athene Seyler, adding: 'Not you, Athene. Another Athene.' To John Osborne he once lamented 'that terribly boring play – oh, of course, you wrote it.'

He got on much better with Vivien Leigh than with her husband – they were both far more widely read than Olivier, and both loved gossip. Olivier sometimes begged him to come to Notley to reason with her, saying he was the only person she would listen to.

In *Twelfth Night*, Olivier took away from Gielgud the authority that a director needs, leading the rest of the cast in mocking him. He was helped by Gielgud's stream of new ideas, and his occasional indecision, leading to changes of moves. Trader Faulkner, who played Sebastian, afterwards told a typical story. Gielgud told him to hold his sword in the other hand, and Olivier said to him: *Trader, baby, I have to admire the way you're not kicking him up the arse.* He also rehearsed Vivien Leigh privately, teaching her to play Viola entirely differently from the way Gielgud wanted her played. He was, perhaps, exercising the only sort of authority left him with his wife. Outside their work, she was completely beyond his control. Inside it, he could dominate her, but only at the expense of marginalising the director.

It came to a dreadful climax at the dress rehearsal. Gielgud wanted to change some moves. Olivier, having first cleared what he was going to do with Glen Byam Shaw, the director of the company, said, in front of all the actors: *Darling John, please go for a walk along the river and let us just get on with it.* Utterly humiliated, Gielgud did as he was bid. Olivier claimed that all he was doing was rescuing the production from Gielgud's indecision, and that he changed nothing of what Gielgud had done. Gielgud discreetly never commented further than to say: 'I wouldn't put it quite that way.'

The Stratford season was a triumph professionally, and a miserable experience personally for both Olivier and his wife. His next enterprise made him money, but did nothing for his reputation. Marilyn Monroe, determined to establish herself as a serious actress and not just an American sex goddess, had decided that the way to do it was to work with Olivier. She had even chosen the play, Terence Rattigan's *The Sleeping Prince*, in which Olivier and Leigh had played the two main parts in the theatre. So for him to play it on film opposite another actress, let alone one whose body was considered her main asset, was a hurtful snub to his wife. But directing and playing opposite one of the world's most famous film stars was a lure Olivier found irresistible.

The set was not a happy place. Olivier thought Monroe desperately needed direction but was not willing to take it from him. Monroe never took a shine to Olivier the man, much as she had

Olivier and Marilyn Monroe during the filming of The Prince and the Showgirl

admired the great actor from afar; she found him overbearing and intimidating, and preferred to take advice from a woman friend she had brought with her – advice Olivier considered pretentious and worthless, based on the American acting scheme called The Method, which Olivier despised. And he could not bear her habit of arriving late on set. *Why can't you come on time, for fuck's sake?* he once shouted at her, and she replied sweetly: 'Oh, do they use that word in England too?'

Olivier, who had been flattered at first because the mega-star wanted him to direct her, concluded contemptuously that Monroe was not an actress but a model. Vivien, when she came to the set, put everyone on edge with her jealousy and resentment, announced she was pregnant, left the Noel Coward play she had taken on two weeks early, much to Coward's disgust, and miscarried. The Monroe-Olivier film, renamed *The Prince and the Showgirl*, was not anything like as bad as it might have been, but it was not especially good either.

Olivier had proved to all the world that he was still the great Shakespearean actor of his generation, but his life was a mess and there was something missing professionally. He had not caught up with the mid fifties, when Britain was starting to come out from under the shadow of the war. He needed something new. And in 1956, he met the young man who was to give it to him.

Enter John Osborne

At first, when 27-year-old John Osborne burst on the world in 1956, Laurence Olivier could not see what all the fuss was about.

He was not alone. Looking back, we can see 1956 as the year the world changed, the hinge of the whole twentieth century, and John Osborne as a key spokesman of a new generation. It was the year Britain invaded Suez and learned belatedly that she was not a world power. A curt instruction from US President Eisenhower to the British Prime Minister Anthony Eden to give up the invasion or face ruin forced Britain to face the finality of the wartime settlement in which it was financially and militarily a vassal of the USA.

It was also the year the Soviet Union invaded Hungary, a brutal affirmation of force which ensured that communism suddenly no longer looked like a beacon of hope in an unfair capitalist world. Communism began to look like yet another oppressor, and the sons and daughters of young idealists who had turned to it in the thirties and forties had to look elsewhere for hope and for inspiration.

But it was also the time when the young were beginning to rebel against the austerity and grey conformity of the immediate post-war years. 1956 was the parent to the sixties, and it was the year the Royal Court theatre opened under George Devine. For the first time, the tight world of West End theatre was kicked open, for new forms of theatre, in a different part of the capital.

Devine opened the theatre with the first play of the new generation, *Look Back in Anger*, marking the end of what Kenneth

John Osborne and Jill Bennett

Tynan once called the 'dododramas' taking place in Colonel Bulstrode's library somewhere in Hampshire. Plays were no longer to be about the rich and middle class, but about the poor too, and the set of *Look Back in Anger* was a cheap, dreary room dominated by an ironing board. It was the start of the era of what was derisively called 'kitchen sink' theatre by its enemies.

And when Laurence Olivier, now pushing 50, went to see the play, when he heard Jimmy Porter shout the anguished cry of his generation 'There are no great brave causes left' – the cry of a generation which could not go and fight for socialism and democracy in Spain, as Jimmy Porter's father had done – Olivier did not know what the man was talking about. He had no idea of the flowering of great brave causes this presaged, from the Campaign for Nuclear Disarmament to Anti-Apartheid – and would not have thought much of them if he had.

He was not alone. His old friend and contemporary, the playwright Terence Rattigan almost walked out after the first act on the first night, and when he emerged from the theatre he told waiting journalists that the play should really have been called *Look Ma, I'm not Terence Rattigan*. He had earlier urged George Devine not to stage it at all, insisting that it would never work in the theatre. Playwriting as a formal craft, plays with a set structure, tracing the emotional lives of the upper and middle classes – these were what Rattigan knew well and did perfectly.

Four years later, in 1960, Rattigan was still saying 'I'm pretty sure it won't survive.' By then he knew what he was up against, adding: 'I'm prejudiced because if it does survive, I know I won't.' He had once described the audience member whom, he thought, no playwright dared upset: 'That nice, respectable, middle-class, middle-aged lady.' He was wrong. The new wave did survive, and Rattigan's work went into a lengthy eclipse from which it is only now, half a century later, beginning to emerge – and we are finding, to our surprise, that he was a better and braver playwright than we gave him credit for, and probably more instinctively radical than John Osborne.

By contrast, Olivier's delicate political antennae caught the new mood quickly. He did not intellectualise about it, as Rattigan had. He was not an intellectual. But neither was he the average middle-aged man. His brain never became sclerotic. Despite his near-contempt for Marilyn Monroe he liked and respected her husband, the great American playwright Arthur Miller, and when Miller came to London and said he would like to see the new play which had 'wiped the smugness off the frivolous face of English theatre' according to John Lahr in the *New York Times Book Review*, Olivier agreed to give it a second try.

After the first act Miller said: 'God, Larry, you're wrong, this is great stuff.' At the Royal Court, Olivier was surrounded by young actors – often a new sort of actor, for the profession was more open than it had been in Olivier's day to those without cut-glass public school accents. And the great actor suddenly felt old, stuffy, establishment. He ached for something new to happen, for a change from the pattern of his work which he described as *a bit deadly – a classical or semi-classical film, a play or two at Stratford, or a nine month run in the West End.*

So when he met John Osborne, he asked the young writer if he might think about writing a play with him in mind. Osborne was delighted and flattered, and within what seemed to Olivier

Olivier in a film still from *The Entertainer*

to be an amazingly short time, the first act of *The Entertainer* arrived. Olivier thought it had been written specially for him, though Osborne says the inspiration came from seeing Max Miller on stage, and he only offered to Olivier afterwards. At all events, Olivier read it, and said at once that he would take the part of Archie Rice at the Royal Court. It changed his life.

Archie Rice is a washed-up stand-up comic in the dusty, depressing dying days of music hall, tap-dancing on windswept piers in three-quarters empty theatres – getting his laughs at his own predicament, as he looks sadly skywards after a thin audience reaction and says: 'Don't laugh too loud, it's a very old building.' Olivier, in his usual manner, researched the part carefully, travelling with Osborne to the few remaining musical halls, learning to tap-dance, learning how to deliver stand-up patter perfectly – and then learning to do it badly, for part of the play's tragedy is that Archie is not very good. In 1957 he performed it at the Royal Court, then transferred to a much bigger theatre, the Palace, then on tour for a month, then back to the Palace again.

And then, in 1959, they filmed it, and the film is with us still, testament to the fact that Olivier could do something new when he was 50 and be the same great actor who had played Hamlet, Macbeth and Heathcliff. Olivier always thought of Archie Rice as his greatest achievement, and he put it down to the fact that *I know that man – I know him better than he knows himself.* He meant, not just that he had met dozens of Archie Rices in dressing rooms during his long career, but that in a sense he was Archie Rice: a man who had played a part so long that he had forgotten who he was. He knew what Archie meant when he said: 'I'm dead behind those eyes – I don't feel a thing.' *It's really me, isn't it?* he once said to John Osborne.

And it was. Archie Rice was everything Olivier would have

been without his prodigious talent: a man who never felt quite real except when he was on a stage, a serial adulterer, and camp as a row of tents.

The Entertainer, set in 1956 during the Suez crisis, is in its way an even more political play than *Look Back in Anger*. It is not just about the death of music hall, but the death of the England in which music hall had flourished: an England in which Archie Rice's father, Billy Rice, could carry audiences with him while he sang songs pleading with the government to keep up a strong navy; an England where a young man off to fight in the useless Suez venture (and, as it turns out, to die there) can say to his sister: 'Life isn't as bad as all that, and even if it is, there's nothing we can do about it.' Both those Englands were dying, and John Osborne was dancing a jig at their funeral.

How much of that did Olivier see? Probably not all of it, but it was the end of the old Olivier. This was an Olivier engaging with the concerns and emotions of Britain as the fifties drew to its close. From this drab, grey decade emerged new playwrights like Osborne and Arnold Wesker, symbols of a new and more colourful future. They were young men, tired of the constraints and compromises of the post-war years, and Olivier was engaging with them in a way that Richardson and Gielgud were not, yet. What Osborne was to Olivier, Robert Bolt was to be for Richardson and Alan Bennett for Gielgud; but that was a long way away. In 1957 only Laurence Olivier had engaged with the new mood.

Thank you, he wrote to John Osborne the day it opened, *for the thrilling and lovely play which will no doubt be in the same Reps Theatre as The Cherry Orchard and The School for Scandal before the century is out. Thank you for the most deeply engaging part, perhaps barring only Macbeth and Lear that I can remember – certainly the most enjoyable. I thank you for the play with all my heart, and for the pride it gives me to be in it, and for the joy of playing it. Hope I don't fuck it up for you tonight.*

But he was not just renewed as an actor in 1957. *The Entertainer* also saw the final parting with Vivien Leigh. And the same period saw his emergence as the great theatrical statesman of his time, a political mover and shaker as no British actor has ever been, before or since.

I thank you for the play with all my heart, and for the pride it gives me to be in it, and for the joy of playing it. Hope I don't fuck it up for you tonight.

Laurence Olivier to John Osborne on the day The Entertainer opened.

With Vivien, there was a brief resurgence of passion. He had become quite unable to make love to her, but his affairs with young actresses cured him. He took his renewed sexual health back to his wife, but it was too late for both of them. For her, love had turned to need and dependency. He vetoed the suggestion that she should play his wife in *The Entertainer*, partly because Osborne was against it, partly perhaps because he may genuinely have believed what he said, that at 43 she was too young and beautiful to play a tired matron of 60; but certainly partly because he saw that Vivien was not to be a part of his new life: she was part of his past. When it came to casting Archie Rice's daughter he rubbed salt in the wound by insisting on having Dorothy Tutin, with whom, he now told Vivien, he had fallen in love. Vivien would arrive unannounced at rehearsals and sit in the dress circle with her chauffeur behind her. Her presence was, John Osborne wrote, 'as distracting as an underwear advertisement at a Lesbians for Peace meeting.' Osborne could sense her loneliness, her sense of loss and exclusion from the great gamble of her husband's life.

Olivier was working very hard as usual – he was to do the play for five weeks in the spring before his summer commitment to revive *Titus Andronicus* – and she insisted on late supper parties and all-night drinking sessions with friends every night. She was demanding his attention all the time, creating dreadful scenes in front of guests to get it, and drinking far too much, though her doctor insisted that she was not turning into an alcoholic – perhaps because if she was an alcoholic, he could not continue to give her ECT. 'Once' writes Donald Spoto 'he had needed her adoration and her dependence; now he resented it.'

Olivier and Vivien tormented each other for months until one night, when she would not let him sleep and hit him across the face with a cold, wet flannel every time he closed his eyes, the anger burst out of him. They hit and screamed at each other with rage. She ended up with a gash above her left eye which caused her to wear an eyepatch for some days – she told the press it was the result of an insect bite. He knew they had to live apart.

Vivien went on holiday with her former husband, Leigh Holman, and their 23-year-old daughter Suzanne. He took his son Tarquin, now 20, on holiday to Scotland, but father and son found, to Olivier's distress, that after all those years apart, they had little to say to each other – especially since Olivier, still obsessively working, spent much of the time searching out locations for the film of *Macbeth* which was never made.

Meanwhile Olivier grew as something he had never intended to be, and probably never thought he was – a politician. He had something few actors have: instinctive political skill. I do not mean he understood politics, or held informed political views, for he did not. But he had instinctive political skill, which is far more important to political success than knowledge. He knew how to handle people, how much to tell them, what to keep to himself. And at the end of the 1950s, over two issues – the fate of his old theatre, the St James's and the proposed National Theatre – he showed himself to have not only acute political instincts, but something much less attractive – a strong sense of realpolitik, an understanding of what battles were winnable and what were unwinnable, and a determination only to fight the former.

In 1956 a building speculator, who had bought the freehold,

obtained permission from the London County Council to demolish the St James's Theatre and replace it with an office block as soon as the Oliviers' lease had run out. Vivien Leigh spearheaded the campaign to save the theatre, and enlisted the support of the actors' trade union Equity. She and Equity organised street marches. Vivien even breached parliamentary protocol by protesting during a debate in the House of Lords, and was escorted out. Her psychiatrist added this to the list of arguments proving she was mad, though if making a scene over an issue which you feel passionate about is madness, there are many of us who could not escape the diagnosis.

Olivier's reaction is interesting. His political antennae told him that the battle was doomed before it started. He was embarrassed by his wife's performance in the House of Lords. *Gallant speeches were made*, he wrote disparagingly in his memoirs. *I, of course, knew that the efforts were quite futile, and Equity did too. But I seemed to be stuck with going along with the ludicrous farce; I was in a helpless situation, neither able to have an open confrontation with Vivien on such an issue, nor to look unwilling to march to save my own theatre. I just had to allow myself to be swung along with the tide.*

On the night of 27 July 1957 the curtain of the St James's Theatre fell for the last time. In November the contents of the theatre were sold by auction. In December it was knocked down. The one success of the campaign was an announcement that in future the London County Council would not allow a live theatre to be demolished in central London unless there was a replacement in the development plans.

The new office block, called St James's House, was completed in 1959. The new owners incorporated sculptures of the greatest figures of its history: Gilbert Miller, George Alexander, Oscar Wilde and the Oliviers.

As to the proposed National Theatre, Olivier had kept a finger in the project for years, sitting on what was called the building committee, which hardly ever met, while never being quite sure whether he approved of it. He at least half-shared the view of some artists that a national, institutional theatre was bound to be unimaginative and uncreative, but he never made the political error of going public, as John Gielgud had done. Gielgud wrote in the *Daily Telegraph* that the proposed National Theatre 'should not waste money on a vast new building; it should not limit itself to just Shakespeare and popular hits . . .' Gielgud became a troublesome outsider to the establishment folk with the power, but Olivier in 1956 became one of the project's trustees. As the project gathered momentum, Olivier went with the political flow. Four years later he became its first director. He knew, instinctively, what the best politicians know: when a bandwagon is on the move, jump aboard.

None of this would have been possible if he had not been almost unbearably discreet about his private life. Dorothy Tutin's parents, seeing an ugly divorce on the horizon, persuaded her and Olivier to end the relationship. She withdrew from the cast of *The Entertainer*, and her part – and quite soon her place in Olivier's life – was taken by one of the Royal Court's lively young people, Joan Plowright.

Plowright was as different from Vivien Leigh as it was possible to be. A happy, secure childhood had left her cheerful, optimistic, stable and down-to-earth. Born in 1929, her father was the editor of the *Lincolnshire Star*. The family moved to Scunthorpe in 1931 where her father took on the editorship of a bigger paper, the *Scunthorpe and Fordingham Star*. Her mother was the mainstay of local amateur dramatics, and introduced Joan to acting, which Joan knew at once was what she wanted to spend her life doing. She won a place at the Old Vic Theatre School in London, where one of her teachers was George Devine, already a respected theatre director. By 1956 she was an established and successful actress working under Devine's direction at the Royal

Court. She was always grateful to Devine, who 'was entirely responsible for transforming me from an actress contracted to "play as cast" into a leading player with a choice of scripts.'

She met Olivier when he first started coming to the Royal Court. He and Vivien came backstage to congratulate her on her first starring part there, in *The Country Wife*. He records that he must have represented everything Joan and others were trying to change in the theatre: *I was titled, necessarily self-satisfied, pompous, patronising, having obviously come to visit in a spirit of condescension.* But he was wrong, says Plowright: 'We were very pleased that he was coming to see us at work. There may have been a few mutterings about the Establishment "joining because they couldn't beat 'em" but they certainly didn't come from the actors.'

They were all, she says, delighted that he was working with them in *The Entertainer*. But she was not at all sure about the offer to take over the part of his daughter when Dorothy Tutin gave it

Olivier sits with Joan Plowright during a performance of *The Entertainer*

up. She did not think it was much of a part. Part of the attraction was the chance of working with Olivier. 'No other actor in the country is such a draw at the box office' she wrote to her parents, and she adds in her memoirs: 'He was bristling with energy and his smile was full of mischief; it was as though he had been let off a leash. He obviously adored playing Archie Rice whom he liked to claim was nearer to him than any part he had ever played. Rehearsing in an open-necked shirt with braces holding up his trousers, he had banished all traces of that titled gentlemen of the Establishment. He was simply an actor among actors, but one of such extraordinary accomplishment, and with such electricity crackling around him, that I was both exhilarated and exhausted by the end of the day.' But – an awkward throwback to his days working with Vivien, had Joan but known it – she found that he and the director, Tony Richardson, were giving her conflicting advice.

She, too, was married, but her marriage was under strain because she was never at home, working six full days a week and often spending Sundays at lunch with theatrical friends whom her husband hardly knew. 'My girlhood dreams' she wrote 'had never been about living my life through a man. I had wanted to be like Florence Nightingale or Saint Joan or Odette of the French Resistance whose lives seems so exciting and purposeful and fulfilled; or of course to be an actress, and able to play them all on stage.' Yet with Olivier she was 'spellbound by the flirtatious charm being directed like a laser beam towards me, even though I knew that my predecessor [Dorothy Tutin] had been the target before me.'

Even more, she was 'touched by the bleakness in his face when he wasn't acting or flirting; by the way Archie's cynicism and gallows humour came so easily to him; and by his admission that his only anchor in life now was the theatre, where he could "knock their eyes out" with his performances and forget about finding happiness in any other form.' She did not want to be just the latest of his conquests, and she made him work for her attention, but later on she wrote to him: 'I want my love to bring you happiness and peace – more than it is doing at the moment. I do not know how I can ever bring you relief from pain – I met you too late for that and you will always have a certain grief that I can do nothing about. But I'll do all I can, I love you with such an aching love . . .'

They took *The Entertainer* to Broadway, and there, for four months, with Vivien and Joan's husband Roger Gage on the other side of the Atlantic, they could spend long hours together. By the end they knew they were determined to spend their lives together.

Separation from Joan's husband was easy – they had drifted apart anyway – but Vivien Leigh was a different matter. If he was going to ask for a divorce, Vivien once remarked to another actress, 'why didn't he do it when I had Finchy [Peter Finch] in tow?' She seemed to be making it a condition of the divorce that Finch came back to her, but there was no chance of that. Olivier seemed afraid Vivien would kill herself if he forced the issue, or at least start refusing her medication.

Plowright wrote in her memoirs: 'Perhaps [Vivien] believed that if she held out long enough, I would be unable to endure the kind of life that I was forced to lead and would put an end to the relationship . . . Nobody underestimated the depth of her genuine distress at the break-up of her marriage and the legend, or the effects of the illness; everyone remained deeply sympathetic and gave her all the support and help they possibly could. Nor did they underestimate the strength of her desire to turn the clock back and have things the way they were; and I was warned of the possibility of visitations at home or at the theatre.' What she does not mention is that she told Olivier to end his ten-year relationship with Danny Kaye, or she would leave him; and he did, though he had refused to do so for Vivien.

In the middle of all this came another personal tragedy. In 1958 Olivier's older brother Dickie, who managed the farm at

Notley for Olivier, was diagnosed with leukaemia and died five months later, aged only 54.

Professionally, Olivier had renewed himself, but he was probably unhappier than he had ever been, and full of guilt and self-loathing. He reacted typically by doing all the work one actor could possibly do, and then a little more. Laurence Olivier Productions made a final appearance, managing a couple of unsuccessful London productions, and he directed an unsuccessful production in New York. And he acted: in a television production of Ibsen's *John Gabriel Borkman*, in a New York production of *The Moon and Sixpence* based on Somerset Maugham's novel about Paul Gaugin, in a financially rewarding *Spartacus* in Hollywood, in *Coriolanus* at Stratford. In Ionesco's *Rhinoceros* he repeated his appalling treatment of John Gielgud when Gielgud directed him in Stratford, by undermining the director Orson Welles: taking groups of the cast away and rehearsing them to do the opposite to what Welles wanted them to do, and then sending Welles out of the theatre while he directed himself. *I'm not a nice person* he said about this time. *I can't wait to be this other person for three hours.*

Laurence Olivier's divorce from Vivien Leigh was a mess. Perhaps it was bound to be.

In early 1959, he was in Los Angeles filming *Spartacus*, and due in Stratford in June to start rehearsing *Coriolanus*. Joan Plowright was working in the West End, and rehearsing for *Roots*, another new Royal Court production by another new wave playwright, Arnold Wesker. Wesker offered a far more radical direction for London theatre even than Osborne. One of the first working-class playwrights, an East End Jew from a well-known Communist family, Wesker was the first of the sixties generation of playwrights whose left-wing politics infused their work. *Roots*, set in London's East End just after the Second World War, was the first of the now famous Wesker trilogy which brought to West End theatre a political radicalism which was as foreign to

John Osborne as it was to Laurence Olivier, but which Joan Plowright found tremendously exciting.

Olivier wrote to Vivien from Los Angeles: *. . . I am quite sure in my mind and heart that both are firmly made up not to return to our life together when I come back in June. In fact, I think it best that we do not see each other . . . I think it's time now that we dropped the legend that is being kept up for press and public, and before I return have some statement ready on the true state of affairs.*

The reply was a threat from a close friend of Vivien's, Victor Stiebel. If he refused to see her on his return, she would refuse her medical treatment (he meant, mainly, ECT) and it would make the illness worse. Olivier wrote to Plowright: *When I read that, my heart did not sink, my brain did not reel. I simply felt without causing it or forcing it a complete and solid and cold determination even while reading it, and then felt lighter and lighter than for ages – isn't that curious?* And as a symbol of his new mood, he gave up drinking for a whole year. It was a big step for a man who, while never an alcoholic, had leaned more and more on alcohol as overwork and personal troubles threatened to overwhelm him. *Never thought I'd be able to endure it*, he wrote to Joan. *The worst is when you first get there and need something to get you going, to conquer the shyness and tide you over that dreadful stretch before dinner.*

Joan heard from mutual friends that Vivien was in a dreadfully self-destructive state, though she also knew that there was a new man in Vivien's life, an actor called Jack Merivale. Joan and Olivier should not meet, she decided, until they had to meet professionally in October to film *The Entertainer*: 'It would sap our strength and integrity and finally we would make some silly mistake, or take a risk that would land us in an awful, undignified mess.' Olivier must withdraw his decision not to meet his wife when he returned from Los Angeles. Vivien should meet Olivier at the airport with some friends, they could have dinner and Olivier could then leave for Stratford.

He hated it, but agreed. She assuaged her guilt about Vivien Leigh by reminding herself that she would happily have gone off with Peter Finch, if he would have had her. At the end of 1959 Olivier went to New York to direct the film *The Tumbler*. He wrote to Plowright:

. . . I worship you so my darling, darling Joanie. Oh forgive me the pain and anxiety I have caused you . . . My love. My Darling. My girl. Child of God. Wumpy Scrumpy . . . It's odd that Joan Plowright decided to put so much of their toe-curling baby talk into her memoirs. She wrote back: 'I had such a beautiful letter from you this morning, full of Scrumpys and Wumpys, very sexy sort of letter and it made me so happy I've had a song in my heart all day long. Oh God, I do love you, love you so . . .'

Vivien still seemed determined to keep him. She asked Rachel Kempson to 'please ask Larry just to have an affair with Joan – I won't mind – if only he won't leave me.' But shortly before Olivier returned to England, Vivien arrived in New York to star in a Broadway musical, and she and Jack Merivale took an apartment. They seemed happy together, and she told Olivier she was in love with Merivale: 'I have found someone kind and dear who takes good care of me.'

He wrote to Joan from the boat back in 1960, after *The Tumbler* opened and he had left Vivien working in New York:

. . . I've just come in from throwing your letters over the side and my heart is still stabbed with the pain of it . . . It felt more than anything just vandalous to throw away such beauty, such precious heartbeats, such a history of love, gallantry, patience and heaven-sent understanding – but there, we said we would, and I have. She did not throw away his letters – 'but then' she explains in her memoirs 'I was living at home and had a safe place to keep them.'

All this care was in vain. He wrote to Vivien from England – a letter which is unsurprisingly omitted from his and Joan Plowright's voluminous published correspondence: *I am bored with the legend of the Oliviers.* Her reply was devastating. Early in the morning of Olivier's 53rd birthday, 22 May 1960, Vivien Leigh issued a press statement in New York which read:

'Lady Olivier wishes to say that Sir Laurence has asked for a divorce in order to marry Miss Joan Plowright. She will naturally do whatever he wishes.' The ambiguity – does 'she' mean Vivien or Joan? – was probably deliberate. Under the divorce laws as they then stood, this statement would make a divorce harder to get, for there was no such thing as an agreed divorce: someone had to be at fault.

At dawn the press pack gathered outside the London homes of Joan Plowright and Laurence Olivier. She was forced to withdraw from the play she was in, fearful not just of the press but of public fury. We can judge it by the fact that her friend Maggie Smith was hoping to buy a small house from a lady who, when the news broke, said: 'You're not a friend of that Joan Plowright, are you' – and refused to sell her the house. But Joan Plowright did open in a revival of *Roots* the next month: 'The audience at the Royal Court was a sympathetic one, [but] I made my first entrance in fear and trembling, not knowing what to expect; but nobody threw anything or heckled me from the gallery.'

Jack Merivale wrote to Olivier explaining the circumstances of the issue of Vivien's press release, saying she had been talked into it by a journalist she knew and had not been rational at the time. It was not done 'vindictively or with calculation.' He added: 'I have to report that we are wonderfully happy together . . . I am certain that there is a wealth of happiness for us in a life together and these are riches we intend to enjoy.'

Olivier knew that he was far from guiltless. He had welcomed her love as balm for his ego, enjoyed and used the legend of the Oliviers; and it had turned sour on him, because he was dealing with a fragile, insecure woman who was increasingly drinking far too much. As for Vivien Leigh's so-called madness, Noel Coward seems to have had that in perspective:

'I suspect there is far less genuine mental instability about it than most people seem to think [and] that all this disgraceful carry-on is really a vino veritas condition. She has always been spoilt and when she fails to get her own way she takes to the bottle and goes berserk.' The insistence of her husband and her doctors on repeated doses of ECT seems to have been at best misguided.

Olivier and Plowright went to New York, she to play in another Royal Court discovery, *A Taste of Honey* by Shelagh Delaney, he to play the archbishop in Jean Anouilh's *Beckett*. In London, Roger Gage was granted a divorce on the grounds of Joan Plowright's adultery with Sir Laurence Olivier, and Vivien Leigh was granted a divorce on the same grounds. Just two weeks later, Olivier and Plowright were married on 17 March 1961, evading the press in Wilton, Connecticut, and the news did not leak until a day or two later. 'We didn't want all the legend stuff' Joan Plowright wrote later. 'He had had it and didn't want it any longer, and I had never had it and didn't like it anyway.' But she was, nonetheless, a professional asset, just as Jill Esmond and Vivien Leigh had been: a young actress in touch with the new movement in the theatre in a way that he could never quite be. And crucially, though much younger than Olivier, she reminded him of his mother.

They started at once to try to have a baby, consulting the best gynaecologists New York could offer. 'Larry insisted' writes Plowright 'on employing the old method of holding me upside down on the bed so that "none of the little buggers can escape."' Richard Kerr Olivier was born on 3 December.

The National Theatre

About the time his son was being born, Olivier was offered a job that he knew at once was exactly what he wanted.

Professionally, he had been drifting since *The Entertainer*. Now a new theatre was to be built in Chichester, and the trustees asked Olivier to run it, promising complete artistic freedom. He could select the plays he wanted, act in whatever he wanted, direct whatever he wanted. And best of all, with the National Theatre project looking at last as though it were about to become reality, Chichester would give him exactly the experience he needed to be first choice to run the NT. He could show he had successfully run a subsidised theatre, and he would have experience of an open stage, which was being planned for the National; for the Chichester stage was to be surrounded on three sides by the audience.

The theatre was just a building site and a set of architects' plans – but what plans! *There could be no better, cleaner, more economical shape for a single-walled auditorium* he wrote in his memoirs, adding: *How lucky can you be? . . . A new home life and an entirely new profession, at my time of life.*

He assembled a company which included some of the biggest names in British theatre, all working for very low salaries. Olivier was more relaxed, and his style more informal, than any of them could remember, partly because Joan Plowright would not have tolerated the regal theatrical airs which Laurence and Vivien Olivier had given themselves.

Typically, he decided to direct the first three Chichester productions himself. One was to be *Uncle Vanya,* with Michael Redgrave as Vanya, Olivier himself as Astrov (he had played the same part at the Old Vic in 1945), Sybil Thorndike and Lewis Casson, and Joan Plowright. *Uncle Vanya* was well received, but his other productions in that first season, two plays dragged from obscurity after research among recondite dramatic literature at the British Museum, were not. Nonetheless, the Chichester Theatre was launched on sound foundations.

Joan Plowright was pregnant again, and she and Olivier bought a house in Brighton – good and big, but with none of the pretensions of Notley. Brighton was convenient for both Chichester and London, and he capped his new life by a set of new year's resolutions on 1 January 1963. He gave up alcohol again for a year – or rather, until 24 December: 'a drinker's year' he called it. He modified his diet, and each morning put on a tracksuit and ran two miles along the Brighton promenade, soon adding weightlifting three times a week.

On 10 January his daughter Tamsin was born. By then he had taken on the biggest challenge of his life.

The idea of a national theatre had been around for 100 years. A site had even been bought in 1937, but war came before anything could be built on it. After the war, the London County Council earmarked some land on the south bank of the Thames, and in 1962 the NT company was formed. Olivier became its first director, and the plan was that the building would be up within three or four years, though in fact it took another 14 years. Until it had its own building, the company would perform at the Old Vic.

But even more than a building, it needed certainty about its role. Peter Hall had been building up the Royal Shakespeare Company at Stratford for two years, and had found it a London home at the Aldwych Theatre. The NT had to show quickly that it was not simply duplicating Hall's efforts.

As soon as Olivier's appointment was public knowledge, he received a letter from Vivien Leigh's old nemesis Kenneth Tynan, now the drama critic of the *Observer* and increasingly a man to be feared in theatrical circles. Could he come and be Olivier's literary manager? (He used the Brechtian word dramaturg.) In this role he would help with selection of plays, casting, publicity and long-term planning.

Despite Tynan's treatment of Vivien Leigh, and his tirade against Olivier's work at Chichester, Olivier admired him. Olivier was also sufficiently politically astute and unsentimental to have made an effort with the man who was emerging as the critic of the John Osborne generation, ready to do to theatre criticism what Osborne had done for playwriting; and who, when he chose, could do an actor or director great harm. Yet John Osborne himself had little but contempt for Tynan. Where Olivier saw in Tynan a well-stocked mind combined with a modern viewpoint, Osborne – who like Tynan was two decades younger than Olivier and very well read, a man of Tynan's generation and background – saw simply a superficial sense of what was fashionable.

Olivier thought the critic better educated than he was himself. New directors were coming out of the universities, instead of emerging, as Olivier and his generation had done, from the upper reaches of the acting profession. Peter Hall from Cambridge and Peter Brook from Oxford may have had less feel for the theatre than Olivier, but they had greater academic knowledge about it. It was essentially a post-war phenomenon, and Olivier may have felt that he needed Tynan's cerebral quality at his elbow.

Joan Plowright was an influence too. She thought it would be better, in Lyndon Johnson's famous phrase, to have Tynan inside the tent pissing out rather than outside pissing in; and that Tynan's presence would ensure Olivier was not seen as a stuffy representative of the old school.

It must have been another dagger in Vivien Leigh's heart. Given Tynan's vigorous and sustained assault on her reputation, it surely seemed to her like a betrayal. She also seems to have believed that Tynan took the place in her former husband's life previously occupied by Noel Coward and Danny Kaye. She may even have been right. Tynan's sexual tastes were primarily heterosexual – he seems to have enjoyed especially spanking women. But John Gielgud for one was sure Tynan had a crush on Olivier, and Olivier found Tynan's outrageousness entertaining in the same way as he had found Danny Kaye's. NT colleagues saw what seemed like flirtatiousness between them.

The only two men who could tell us for certain, Olivier and Tynan, are dead – but we do know that when, years later, Tynan talked of writing a biography of Olivier, his old boss exploded in fury, refused to be interviewed, and asked all his friends to have nothing to do with it. Tynan was forced to abandon the project. It is hard to see why Olivier would have been quite as angry unless there was something in it he did not want made public.

Whatever the personal ramifications, John Osborne was only one of those who thought the professional result disastrous, with Olivier subordinating his own judgement of plays to that of his literary manager. Tynan became Olivier's principal lieutenant, and even attended board meetings, though without a vote.

For his two associate directors, Olivier went to the Royal Court, which ensured he got young, new talent – William Gaskill and John Dexter. Gaskill soon left, because Tynan was being allowed to dictate casts and was insisting on stars: he returned to the Royal Court where he eventually became artistic director. Dexter lasted a little longer, but after a huge row with Olivier over Dexter's plans for an all-male *As You Like It*, left for New York.

Similarly for his 50 or so actors, Olivier wanted rising young talent, not the stars of his generation. He did not go to old friends, but to younger actors, sometimes suggested by Joan Plowright. John Gielgud and Ralph Richardson were not invited to join the company. Tynan did try to recruit Alec Guinness, but Guinness did not want to work under Olivier – he felt, according to his biographer Garry O'Connor, that Olivier 'sapped the energy of other people and lived off it.' Gielgud came in briefly in a small part in an unsuccessful production of Moliere's *Tartuffe* four years later, and did not work for the National again until Olivier left. Richardson had nothing to do with the National until Olivier left.

Despite wanting to be up-to-the-minute, Olivier as director of the National Theatre was more than ever conscious of being a kind of representative of Englishness, as the Australians had seen him on that post-war Antipodean tour. The day after President Kennedy was assassinated in 1963, at the end of the matinee of *Uncle Vanya*, Olivier stepped forward, held up his hand, and asked that there should be no applause: instead the audience should stand in silence for two minutes, at the end of which the silence was broken by the strains of *The Star Spangled Banner*. Two years later, for Winston Churchill's funeral in January 1965, he spoke the commentary for the ITV coverage, which he considered a great honour, and he was pleased that more people watched ITV than the BBC.

One of the big new names he brought in was Peter O'Toole, who played Hamlet in the new NT company's first production, a full, uncut version of the play, which lasted no less than five hours. It was not entirely a success, but the season was saved because Olivier, who was still the director at Chichester and had made the management of Chichester part of the National's responsibility, brought in the Shaw and Chekhov plays he had staged there.

Olivier decided to take for himself the next great Shakespeare role at the National Theatre: Othello. He prepared for it with his usual physical and mental thoroughness. There was a vicious weightlifting regime, as well as a lot of roaring at cows in the countryside, to expand his ribcage and get the vocal depth and volume – he succeeded in lowering his voice by a full octave. He did what he always did – finding the character from the outside, beginning with external characteristics. He rejected the usual compromise of making Othello coffee-coloured: he wanted him to be deeply black. 'I had to feel black down to my soul. I had to look out from a black man's world' he said. It took him three hours to make up for every performance, starting by shaving his chest, arms and legs and then staining his whole body, painting his fingernails, coating the inside of his mouth. It took another two hours to take it all off afterwards. He concerned himself with the tiniest details. What were his bare feet doing while he was speaking? To keep them from unwanted curling, when he walked backstage before his entrance, he kept each foot flat to the ground as it hit the floor, stiffening the foot so that his toes would stay still on stage. The walk also introduced the swaying hips which were a feature of his performance.

The performance fully justified all the effort that had gone into it, and received rave notices and packed houses.

Hamlet and *Othello* were two of no less than 10 plays in the first season of the NT, with a different play every night and even a changeover between matinee and evening performances. Most productions in its first few seasons attracted admiration, and the choice of plays was skilful: a small proportion of Shakespeare, some comedy and some farce including a Noel Coward play, and new plays which required more technical and casting resources than the commercial theatre could provide, like John Arden's *Armstrong's Last Goodnight*. In 1967 Olivier brought in a new play by a new, exciting young playwright – Tom Stoppard's *Rosencrantz and Guildenstern are Dead* – straight from the fringe of the Edinburgh Festival.

He prepared for Othello with his usual physical and mental thoroughness. There was a vicious weight-lifting regime, as well as a lot of roaring at cows in the countryside, to expand his ribcage and get the vocal depth and volume – he succeeded in lowering his voice by a full octave.

The first few seasons of the NT were a triumph – and they were Olivier's triumph. 'From Albert Finney and Joan Plowright to Colin Blakely and Geradine McEwan' writes Simon Trussler in the *Illustrated History of British Theatre*, 'from Frank Finlay and Lynn Redgrave to Robert Stephens and Maggie Smith, from Robert Lang and Derek Jacobi to Ronald Pickup and Anthony Hopkins, the roll-call reads as impressively now as it seemed innovative and often type-challenging then.'

At the same time he had his agent put it about that he was available for limited film work, and the offers tumbled in. One of the most memorable was his wonderful short cameo as Sir John French in Richard Attenborough's film of Joan Littlewood's *Oh What a Lovely War*, in which, as he dances a waltz, his dancing partner muses on the name of General Haig. She thinks she's heard it before. 'Whisky' grunts Olivier, and there is a bottomless pit of contempt in the single word. 'Trade?' she asks, shocked. ''Fraid so' grunts Olivier, and you can glimpse a whole world of pre-First World War snobbery.

The National Theatre was proving itself under Olivier's direction, but Olivier was overworking again, and after a while came the reckoning.

He was under strain when Joan Plowright became pregnant for the third time, and found coping with her eventual miscarriage very stressful. His mental state was made worse by two painful confrontations with old friends. First, he fired Michael Redgrave after the actor forgot his lines in *The Master Builder*, and took on the part himself. It was a brutal over-reaction to a minor lapse, which upset Redgrave more than almost anything that had happened to him, for he admired Olivier enormously. Olivier seems wrongly to have assumed Redgrave's problem was caused by drinking too much – in fact, unknown even to Redgrave himself, it was a symptom of the early onset of Parkinson's disease. Both men afterwards subscribed to the myth that Redgrave had left of his own accord.

A publicity still of Olivier from *Oh What a Lovely War*

He then almost got to the point of firing Edith Evans, who was in the National production of *Hay Fever*, which was being directed by Noel Coward himself. The production was tried out in Manchester, and it became clear that Edith Evans was also struggling with her lines and her character. Olivier had mentally given her a day or two to improve, resolving that if she did not, he must fire her too.

And then, a couple of days after Plowright's miscarriage, about to perform Redgrave's part in *The Master Builder* in Manchester, standing in the dressing room which both Redgrave and Evans had used before going on stage and forgetting their lines, feeling guilty about both of them, Olivier thought: *I think I'm too tired to remember it.* With a terrible certainty he knew he was going to dry up on stage that night, forget his lines and be consumed by stage fright. It was the start of a torment that lasted for five years. His company were far more forbearing than he had been with Redgrave and Evans.

The NT went to Moscow and West Berlin in the autumn of 1965 with *Othello, Hobson's Choice* and a Congreve play, *Love for Love*. Moscow made Olivier nervous, for it was where Stanislavsky had taught, and Olivier's way of working still derived from Stanislavsky. The night before an important lunch for the movers and shakers in Soviet culture, he got massively drunk by alternating champagne and vodka, and simply could not get out of bed; Joan Plowright told the assembled company he had collapsed with exhaustion after a hard morning rehearsing. It was something he did occasionally: once at a party at the Chichester theatre he had launched into an abominably rude drunken tirade at the chairman of his board, and had to make the fullest and most obsequious apologies in the morning.

Back in London, Olivier's troubles began to pile up. There was an acrimonious row with Peter Brook, whom he had commissioned to direct *Oedipus* with John Gielgud. Brook had decided that the show should end on a note of forced, vulgar jollity, and he wanted the cast to dance in the aisles, unchoreographed, to a jazzed-up version of *God Save the Queen*. He also wanted a six foot high phallus on the stage. Olivier was horrified – perhaps more than anything at the desecration of the sacred anthem. It would probably be only a little unfair to say that he liked innovation so long as he was in charge and could control it.

But in the end he did not stop Brook – mainly because Kenneth Tynan weighed in on Brook's side, and slyly told Olivier that Brook might make mischief in the newspapers. Olivier, used to getting his own way, felt defeated and demoralised.

Joan's last pregnancy was also difficult, but this time with a happy outcome: their third child, Julie-Kate, was born by caesarean section in July 1966. Like Jill Esmond and Vivien Leigh before her, Plowright found her husband taking charge of her career, not necessarily to her advantage. Bill Gaskill, back at the Royal Court, asked Olivier to allow her to return to the Royal Court for a production of *The Three Sisters* – he knew that Olivier was considering a production of the same play, with her in the cast. Olivier refused; Joan was to be in his production of the same play later on, he said. She wrote in her memoirs that Gaskill's offer was attractive to her: 'I would have loved to have gone back and continued my association with the Royal Court. It would have alleviated some of the burden I carried as the "director's wife" at the National. Larry, however, was adamant that I should wait and do it with him.'

It was not the last time she tried to go back to the Royal Court, or to take other work, and was prevented by her husband; and she eventually got to the stage which neither Jill Esmond nor Vivien Leigh had reached, of deciding to do it anyway and letting him rail.

There was illness. First there was prostate cancer, then, as he was receiving treatment for that, pneumonia, from both of which he briefly thought he might die, and through both of which he did far more work than his doctors wanted him to do. And then, one July morning in 1967, a telephone call from Jack Merivale forced him to confront his past. Vivien Leigh had died in the night, aged only 53.

She had been happy enough with Merivale, though she kept Olivier's photograph at her bedside and constantly re-read his letters to her. She had revived her career in the sixties, starring on screen in *The Roman Spring of Mrs. Stone* (1961) and *Ship of Fools* (1965), and winning a Tony in the Broadway production of *Tovarich* (1963). But her manic-depressive interludes never really left her, nor did her tuberculosis, which is what killed her.

Olivier was in hospital when he took Merivale's call, being treated for the cancer. At once he discharged himself, and rushed to Leigh's home. He felt guilty – no doubt with some cause. But she once told a friend that she would 'rather have lived a short life with Larry than face a long life without him.'

Perhaps he never got over her, any more than she got over him. Years later, a visitor to his home found the 80-year-old Olivier sitting alone, watching Leigh in an old film on television. *This, this was love,* he said, in tears. *This was the real thing.* Tarquin Olivier, Olivier's son from his first marriage, is convinced that Vivien Leigh was and always remained the love of his father's life. He too remembered his father, as an old man, asking, with tears in his eyes, what could have gone wrong with her. The answer, at least in part, lay in himself.

There was more. After Vivien's funeral, Olivier and his friend, agent and adviser Cecil Tennant said a casual goodbye to each other outside St Mary's Catholic Church in London's Cadogan Square. Tennant was killed in a car crash on his way home.

Outwardly, things got better. Oliver's health improved for a while. There were successes at the National, and in 1970 two huge triumphs. On Prime Minister Harold Wilson's recommendation he became the first ever actor peer, and was henceforth known as Lord Olivier. And he chose to play Shylock in Jonathan Miller's production of *The Merchant of Venice*, set in the nineteenth century, with Joan Plowright playing Portia.

He found that he could learn from the young Miller in a way that he could not from directors of his own generation. There was none of the undermining which John Gielgud and Orson Welles had suffered at Olivier's hands. Olivier started rehearsing with a prominent hooked nose, Hassidic curls, a beard, and a thick stage Jewish way of speaking. 'This would have been very vulgar', Miller said years later 'and being Jewish myself I could say to him "Larry, you know this is rather a cliché – not all of us look and sound that way.", Miller got the performance he wanted out of Olivier – something that few other directors had achieved in recent years – though Olivier was sure he had based his final character on his uncle Sidney Olivier. However it was achieved, it was, by all accounts, brilliant.

But Olivier kept the panic away only by using liberal doses of Valium at each performance, and eventually he had to give up the part because of a bout of pleurisy and a thrombosis in his right leg, a blood clot which kept him in bed for six weeks. The doctors told him not to act for a year and to cut down his official commitments. The next year, to add to the painful leg, there was arthritis and a whiplash injury that forced him to wear a neck brace.

None of that stopped him from making his only speech in the House of Lords. The newly-elected Conservative government under Edward Heath wanted to end the practice of trade unions running a closed shop, which ensured that everyone in the business joined the union. This would open actors up to just the sort of exploitation that had existed before Equity, in Olivier's youth, and the Equity official Peter Plouviez, later its general secretary, had little difficulty persuading his most distinguished member to speak against it in the Lords, despite Olivier's instinctive conservatism.

His judgement for plays and directors was starting to desert him. Strange, avant-garde productions of obscure plays, generally championed by Kenneth Tynan, started to overload the National's seasons and undermine its box-office success. But if Tynan was part of the problem, he was also part of the solution. For 1971 he suggested Eugene O'Neill's *Long Day's Journey Into Night* with Olivier in the main part, one of Olivier's greatest performances and a huge success. In 1972 the production of Tom Stoppard's *Jumpers*, the revival of Ben Hecht and Charles MacArthur's *The Front Page*, and Jonathan Miller's production of *The School for Scandal*, were all highly successful and all Tynan's idea.

But by then, the vultures were circling. 1967 – the year of his cancer and of Vivien's death – was also the year in which the relationship between the National Theatre board and its director began to deteriorate. The rift started with Kenneth Tynan's proposal that they do a play by a German playwright, Rolf Hochhuth, called *The Soldiers* – an attack on the Allied bombing of Hamburg and Dresden during the war, and on Olivier's old hero Winston Churchill, the Prime Minister who ordered it. The play also claimed that Churchill arranged for the murder of the Polish General Sikorski, who was killed in an air crash in 1943.

There is a case for saying that the carpet bombing of these cities counts as a war crime. Today it is most often made by German neo-Nazis, which rather undermines it; but in those days it did not have that association.

Olivier did not much like the play, but both Tynan and Plowright did, and he did not want to appear out of touch. *I have been torn*, he rather typically told his board, *between my prejudices as an Englishman and my wishes for the NT as its director.* And for the NT, he wanted, he said, not just to produce the classics, but to produce controversial and innovative new work too. He and Tynan had met the author, and found him prepared to compromise over his script.

Tynan was roasted by the chairman, the experienced politician Oliver Lyttelton, now Lord Chandos, who accused him of misleading the board by suggesting that historians considered Hochhuth's theory at least possible. Hugh Trevor-Roper, for one, did not, said Chandos, from which he deduced that 'the play is based upon a lie.'

The board decided against the play, and the Lord Chamberlain ruled that the play could not be seen without the permission of Winston Churchill's family. Now Lord Chandos had Tynan firmly in his sights. He had probably never liked the man anyway; but Chandos had been a member of the War Cabinet which sanctioned the Dresden bombing, so he was outraged at the attack on a decision in which he had participated. He wanted Tynan's scalp; Tynan at one point suggested that Olivier should resign rather than agree to provide it.

Instead, Olivier, the patient politician, begged for time and patience, but he was still on the defensive over his literary manager more than a year later, when he wrote to Chandos in October 1968: *It did not seem to me that he {Tynan} was given more than a very meagre opportunity to explain himself, and my own reading of this incident was that he was guilty more of over-stating his case than bare dishonesty.* Many of the National Theatre's successes were Tynan's idea, he said, and many of its failures were not Tynan's fault. He would be thoroughly unhappy if the board got rid of Tynan: *I would be quite stricken if a partnership such as this were to be dissolved.*

Chandos was furious, claiming to read in Olivier's letter a suggestion that he and Tynan were as unreliable as each other, and demanding that the letter be withdrawn. Otherwise 'I must reply in full, and that would really cost you some sleep, and perhaps damage our relationship irrevocably.' Olivier withdrew it. Chandos spent a good deal of time closely analysing the meeting, obsessively determined to prove that Tynan had tried to mislead the board. A careful letter from Olivier to the *Times*, defending

Tynan, drew another salvo from Chandos in the same paper, and he wrote to Olivier: '[Tynan] is both dishonest and untruthful, and if you recognise this fact it will save you a lot of tears in the future.' Olivier the naturally gifted politician was up against Chandos the old political hand. He lost the battle over Hochhuth's play, but the war was still in the balance.

Olivier had his revenge, though ostensibly on a different issue. Chandos disagreed with his proposal to bring Joan Plowright into the NT administration. Olivier had a private meeting with the veteran fixer

Joan Plowright at Buckingham Palace with her children Richard and Tamsin

Lord Goodman and the Arts Minister Jennie Lee and told them he could no longer work with Chandos. They fixed it. Chandos only chaired one more board meeting, after which he told Olivier: 'They've decided to get rid of me. I suppose I'm getting on a bit.' Olivier records his own response unblushingly: 'Oh, Oliver, that must seem terribly ungrateful – after all you have done to bring about a National Theatre in our country.' Chandos died two years later.

By the next year, 1970, with its director ill, the NT company was getting restive, and the discontent was leaked to a newspaper. Critics complained that the NT was starting to look stale and uninspired. The director meanwhile was starting to resent his literary manager who had caused him so much trouble. The proposed production of *Guys and Dolls* had to be cancelled because Olivier, who was to play Nathan Detroit, was ill again. When he recovered, they decided to go ahead – and then the board, overruling their director, cancelled it when it was well into rehearsal. Olivier was furious; he called it 'treachery.' There were more company rows, and Joan Plowright decided at last to brave her husband's wrath and leave, committing herself to Chichester, now run by John Clements, for its tenth anniversary season. Her explanation is revealing:

'I needed for a while to be just an actress again; to be offered parts and accept or turn them down on their merits and my own desire to do them, instead of allowing myself to be persuaded into things because John Dexter needed an anchor in his cast, or Paul Schofield would rather have me than Vanessa Redgrave . . . Larry's illnesses had taken their toll and his ideas about a possible successor had not proved acceptable.' She had a thoroughly good time, away from the pressures and the politicking.

Olivier tried out several names as his successor, in particular that of one of his two associate directors, Michael Blakemore – and that of his wife, though Joan Plowright herself did not want the job and knew she was not qualified to do it. But he was half-hearted about it; they rightly thought there was a large part of their director which did not want to go, and another which hoped, quite unrealistically, that he could pass the job onto his wife, as though he were some medieval monarch. So, behind his back, the board took matters into their own hands.

In March 1972, the day he returned from one his lucrative film performances – £20,000 for five days filming Robert Bolt's *Lady Caroline Lamb* – the new chairman, Sir Max Raine, told him that the NT board had decided on his successor: Peter Hall. The decision had been kept secret from Olivier for several months, and now he was expected to keep it from his colleagues. Olivier, furious though he was, did so. Kenneth Tynan and his wife were due for dinner that night, and Olivier insisted that he and Joan must keep the news from him. But a few days later the *Guardian* got the story. Tynan was furious. Hall's appointment, he said, was an 'insane mistake.' Hall felt the same about Tynan. His verdict was: 'Tynan tried to run the National like a Renaissance court, with himself as secretary of state or chief cardinal to Olivier as pope. In gliding around like a not very Machievellian Machiavelli, Tynan was not really very helpful to Larry.'

Olivier and Peter Hall outside the newly-constructed National Theatre in London

The changeover was not easy. Olivier was furious at the underhand way things had been handled. Jonathan Miller spoke to him about it, and later said: 'The putsch was achieved in an appallingly offensive manner . . . He should have been directly involved in the change of administration, and he knew it.' It was done shoddily, in the way that politicians and bureaucrats do things, but perhaps some of the blame rests with the director himself, who simply could not imagine the NT in anyone else's hands and had not therefore established and built up his own successor. Peter Hall's diaries reveal Olivier's constant vacillation about the date of his own departure. But at last, on 2 April 1964, the deed was done. Olivier was not to lead his company to its new theatre, though the main auditorium was to be called the Olivier, and the smaller one became the Lyttleton after his old friend and old enemy Oliver Lyttelton, Lord Chandos. His old chum Ralph Richardson was, however, at last to play a lead part at the National Theatre, which he had never been able to do under Olivier: Peter Hall asked him to play in *John Gabriel Borkman*.

Plowright, feeling a great weight lifted from her shoulders, joined the small company at the Greenwich Theatre, which was run on a shoestring, and enjoyed it so much that she had no hesitation in turning Peter Hall down when he asked her to join his NT company, even though Hall warned her there would not be enough money around to keep these small theatres open.

But the man behind Greenwich, Robin Phillips, was offered a job as artistic director at the Stratford Ontario Theatre in Canada, and without him the Greenwich company would not survive. So Hall had his way: he got Olivier to direct his wife in *Eden End*. Plowright never forgave him, even suggesting that he had recommended Phillips for the Canada job to get him out of the way. For Olivier's other NT swansong he took Joan Plowright's advice, and chose a play by the young left-wing writer Trevor Griffiths, *The Party*, about the state of the British Communist Party, directed by John Dexter.

Olivier had been in the habit of making the occasional film while running the NT, for the money, especially since he now had school fees to pay for his three children. His attitude to paying school fees, given his considerable wealth, seems remarkably stingy: he complained that the level of income tax made it hard to save the money. *The authorities are not touched by this plight, they have no sympathy for our educational ambitions for our children, they want every man-jack of us to love the state school. They refuse to recognise in what shallow waters they flounder, against the flood of intelligent opinion and inclination.* The vast majority of his fellow citizens have, of course, no choice but these state schools which he regarded with such contempt; and those schools would cease to exist if the likes of the Oliviers were not forced to pay income tax.

So now, in the handover period, he brought in extra money by making the film *Sleuth* with Michael Caine; and he also, for the first and only time in his life, made an advertisement, for Polaroid cameras. He stipulated that, while it could be shown in the USA and Europe, it must not be shown in Britain.

Now 65, Olivier had to get used to the deaths of friends. Perhaps the hardest was his old friend and lover Noelie – Noel Coward, who had at last been given a knighthood. *We remember*, wrote Olivier, *his talents, the masterliness and the variety of them, his originality, brilliant wit and understanding . . . With his dazzling prowess as a light comedian, he was the most complete master of the stage in this century, and adored by his friends, and many millions of others.*

I wish I'd known him better

The spirit was as willing as ever, but the flesh in its sixties could not take the knocks any more. An intruder in the Oliviers' home hit him across his nose, causing long-term problems in his right eye. A clumsy dive into the sea on an Italian holiday ricked his back. An unusual and very serious disease of the skin and muscles had him in hospital for 16 weeks, taking massive doses of steroids and being fed intravenously, and looked as though it might well kill him or leave him permanently disabled. The side effects of the steroids included swelling of the legs, a puffy face, severe thirst, mood changes and hallucinations. It left him, for a while, unable to touch anyone without severe pain, but he fought his way nearer to health than anyone could have hoped, and, amazingly, he was able to return to acting, though he was never able to act in the live theatre again.

The honours of a very distinguished elderly gentleman were enormous consolation. He loved honours. From the queen came an Order of Merit; from British Railways, a letter saying that the train which pulled the 12.40 inter-city service from London to Wolverhampton was to be called the Laurence Olivier.

By May 1975, after nearly a year out of action with illness, he was able to work again. He took a very small part in *The Seven Per Cent Solution*, and then started talking with director John Schlesinger about playing the old Nazi torturer in the thriller *Marathon Man*. At lunch to discuss it, according to Schlesinger, 'He was terribly enfeebled, and hearing his very high old man's voice I realised it would be impossible for him to work with us.

But he wanted to know the story, so I went through it with him. His eyes sparkled at the prospect of playing this monstrous villain, and he became very theatrical and a bit camp, insisting how much fun it would be to act this wicked man. And there, right before my eyes, I saw the old actor coming to life, making a recovery!'

Ill and in constant pain though he still was – he still had to remind people not to shake his hand because it was so painful – he nonetheless flew to America and produced a terrifying performance opposite Dustin Hoffman.

There were more films in 1976, as well as the start of a project suggested by Joan's brother David Plowright, controller of programmes for Granada Television. The series was called 'Best Play of 19-', and the idea was for Olivier to produce six plays, each one chosen as the best of any year in the twentieth century. He produced them in his usual way, taking care of every detail himself, no matter how much pain it cost him, and playing cameo parts in some of them.

The Lyttelton Theatre opened in March 1976, and the Olivier in October. He was forced to miss the opening of the Lyttelton, but carefully rehearsed and memorised his speech for the opening of the Olivier, after which he stood and accepted the applause for five minutes. More films followed, and actors and directors on film sets found a lonely and frail elderly man who could not bear for an evening to end, always suggesting another glass of whisky, no matter how early a start was needed the next morning.

Sometimes his fellow actors thought he was starved of affection. He normally travelled alone – Joan Plowright, after ten years living in her husband's shadow, was working hard and enjoying being mistress of her own career. His children were so much younger than him that he felt much more like a grandfather to them than a father, and they remember him exclusively as an ill man.

Increasingly his third marriage was a shell, kept up for appearances and for the children. Partly, according to Plowright, he resented the fact that she was now the one doing most of the work and earning most of the money, though by the standards of most of their fellow citizens they were fabulously wealthy. Olivier had inherited his father's obsessive concern about money, though he had far less cause for it than his father. He frequently reminisced sadly about Vivien.

Joan Plowright was a political radical of the John Osborne generation, he an instinctive conservative from the Terence Rattigan generation, so it was significant that their marital problems came to a head in 1979. This was one of those political hinge years, like 1945 or 1956, when the political landscape shifted. In that year a radical Conservative government came to power, with Mrs Thatcher at the head of it, determined to end the post war consensus around nationalisation and the welfare state. On election night the Oliviers accepted an invitation from Lady Hartwell, wife of the proprietor of the Conservative *Daily Telegraph*. Joan Plowright writes: 'It was upper Tory and upper class, except for occasional interlopers like Tom and Miriam Stoppard, and us, and Lord Goodman.' Of course, Laurence Olivier was not an interloper in that company at all: a Lord, an instinctive Tory, and the product of a public school (albeit a minor one). Neither, come to that, was Tom Stoppard, even more conservative that Olivier and far more committed and cerebral about it. But Joan, perhaps, was; she seems, discreetly, to have shared the horror of the 1956 generation at the rise of Thatcherism, while Olivier, no doubt, rather welcomed it.

But the fundamental problem between them was that, even in old age, Olivier wanted to control. And when Peter Hall offered Joan Plowright the magnificent part of Martha in *Who's Afraid of Virginia Woolf?*, Olivier was furious, telling her she should not do it under any director but him. She did it anyway, and he asked his solicitor to write to her for a divorce – though he thought better of it a few days later. She blamed the extra strain he imposed on her for the fact that her voice gave way after the first few performances, and she had to pull out of the cast. She was bitterly disappointed, the more so when Laurence Olivier attended the *Evening Standard* awards dinner and watched Margaret Tyzack accepting the Best Actress award for the part Joan Plowright had been forced to vacate.

They both thought it was his fault. They were probably right. He went into one of his self-flagellating fits of remorse. She tried to remind herself that she had said she would love him forever, whatever he did. When Olivier's old friend Trader Faulkner wrote to her congratulating her on a performance, she proudly showed the letter to her husband, but instead of congratulating her, he dropped the letter on the table and said: *I must get back on the stage.* He seemed not to be able to bear the idea that she could have successes independently of him. Her career, she must have felt, was something she had to fight her husband for. The next year, 1980, Joan Plowright asked her son Richard Olivier to announce through the family lawyers that she would 'neither attend award functions for her husband nor accompany him on trips.'

Just before the shooting of *The Boys from Brazil*, in which he was to play a Jewish Nazi-hunter modelled on Simon Wiesenthal, he was rushed into hospital again with kidney stones. When he was able to start filming, a couple of months late, he was determined to fulfil the exacting physical demands of the role, even down to the final fight with Gregory Peck. He also wanted a romantic adventure with the actress who coached him in his Viennese accent, Marcella Markham, an idea which did not appeal to her at all.

Some jobs were great professional challenges, some just paid well. One of the latter was Professor van Helsing in *Dracula*, filmed from September 1978 to February 1979, for which Olivier earned nearly $1 million. Another was a taxing $1 million job playing General Macarthur in a film backed by right-wing American evangelists called *Inchon*. Asked why he did this sort of work, he replied: *To pay for three children in school, for a family, and their future. But nothing is beneath me if it pays well. I've earned the right to damn well grab whatever I can in the time I've got left.*

The television serial adaptation of Evelyn Waugh's *Brideshead Revisited* was much less well paid, but much more worthy of his talents. His Lord Marchmain, dying and guilty, ranked among his great performances.

Olivier as Lord Marchmain in the TV adaptation of *Brideshead Revisited*

In March 1980 he settled down to write an autobiography. Another bout of illness had made acting even harder, and he was determined to scupper the proposed biography by Kenneth Tynan. The only acting work which was allowed to interrupt the writing was the offer of a wonderful part in a one-off television play. He played John Mortimer's father Clifford Mortimer, the barrister who dealt with his blindness by ignoring it. He was almost too ill to act: he could not get his cues right, and ended up using huge blackboards off-camera with his lines written on them. He knew he was failing and his distress was painfully obvious. Yet he turned in a fine performance.

The autobiography, *Confessions of an Actor*, published in 1982, turned out to be at times very revealing, at times infuriatingly opaque, and at times self-servingly inaccurate. It is the work of a man who has acquired in old age a pretty realistic assessment of himself: prodigiously talented, painstaking and hard-working, and remarkably selfish and egotistical. The word 'confessions' in the title foreshadows the style, which is that of a high-church Anglican visiting a confessional. He ends the book: *For these, and for all my other sins, which I cannot now remember, I firmly purpose amendment of life and humbly ask pardon of God and of you, Reader, counsel, penance and absolution.*

He had never not acted before in the whole of his adult life. In fact, the actor had become the man – the man who didn't like himself, and who, as he had once put it, couldn't wait to be this other person for three hours. Joan Plowright said: 'He says he's not quite sure when he's acting and when he's not and I can't always tell. It's a bit eerie really.' He added: *I suppose to some degree I am liberated only when acting.* And he also said: *I have to act to breathe, I can only stop if He up there smites me.*

And so, the moment the book was done, he was back at the old trade, producing against the odds his last great performance in one of the big Shakespeare parts. Olivier's film of *King Lear* for Granada, which he could make because he had been planning the project and slowly learning the lines for years, is as good as anything he ever did – the equal of his *Hamlet* or his *Richard III*. Right from the start you know you are watching one of the greatest actors of all time; for in the very first scene, he makes

Lear's extraordinary behaviour believable by a small but utterly human and believable movement. After Goneril (played by his old flame Dorothy Tutin) and Regan have produced their praise, he turns to Cordelia:

> What can you say to draw
> A third more opulent than your sisters? Speak.

And as he says it, he nestles comfortably into his throne, a self-indulgent but hard-earned smile crosses his face, and we know he is visibly preparing to let the warm syrup of her praise wash over him and soothe his troubled, aged loneliness; so that when she refuses to do so, we can almost sympathise with his fury.

He played a series of film cameos, gradually recovering his strength and learning to rely on autocues. There were more deaths to sadden him, more funerals to go to: most importantly his old friend Ralph Richardson, who died after suffering two disabling strokes. When Olivier heard the news, he sat in silence for a while and then started talking at length about John Gielgud.

There were honours – Emmys, *Evening Standard* awards, honorary degrees, Hollywood Golden Globe Awards, all the rest of it – but little seemed to touch his loneliness. In New York, after prolonged and tumultuous applause for him at a star gala, he said proudly *Let's telephone Joanie*. But Joan Plowright's maid told him: 'Lady Olivier says she is at dinner.' Olivier put down the telephone and, according to those who were there, there was shocked silence for a moment. At last Olivier said: *Joan expected me to die when I was seventy. Unfortunately I didn't.*

After *Confessions of an Actor* came another book, *On Acting*. It's a rambling book, offering a few useful points of technique and a lot of musing on his craft.

Acting, he writes in it, *is like the first sip of beer, the one you probably steal as a child, the taste you never forget, it makes such an impression on your palate . . . Acting is often put down by outsiders, who are not interested anyway, as a game played by adults who ought to know better. It is not; it is a great art and, when it is done well, it stands out on its own, supreme and satisfying.*

On Acting also offers the occasional insight into Olivier's mind, which seems to have become increasingly self-righteous with the passing of the years. John Gielgud, he says, is *a very sweet man who is forever saying terrible things about me.* This is quite untrue. Gielgud was always generous in his praise of Olivier, and the jealous and spiteful remarks in their relationship mostly came from Olivier. *I will always be an active actor* he writes in *On Acting, and John a passive one.* This is an extraordinarily unfair and self-serving description of the difference between their two techniques, though the passage goes on to praise Gielgud lavishly.

Acting is like the first sip of beer, the one you probably steal as a child, the taste you never forget, it makes such an impression on your palate.

Laurence Olivier, On Acting.

Gielgud was affronted by *Confessions of an Actor*, not at what was said about him, but at the cruel detail Olivier had included about Vivien Leigh. After reading newspaper extracts, he refused to read the book itself. 'I was really Vivien's friend', he told a journalist. 'I've rarely seen Larry since she died.'

Post-autobiography films included a remarkable portrayal of Rudolf Hess in a story about a plan to smuggle Hess out of Spandau prison – Hess's son Wolf Rudiger Hess said the likeness was uncannily accurate. But his film parts were now mostly lucrative cameos. His growing wealth – far, far more than was required to send his children to even the poshest fee-charging schools, whatever he may have said about the cost – enabled the purchase of a second home in London, a splendid Chelsea mansion.

His memory for recent events was going, he was prone to dizzy spells, he fell over and hurt himself a few times. He talked more and more about Vivien Leigh, seeming to seek reassurance constantly that he had not really treated her so badly. He wanted badly to work, but by the mid 1980s his agent knew it was not possible. He attended plays directed by his son Richard, or in which his daughter Tamsin was acting, and tried to direct the press attention he attracted onto his children. He lived a lot in the past, a place populated by his 'precious mummy' and by Vivien.

In May 1987, there was a gala entertainment at the National to celebrate Olivier's 80th birthday. At the finale his daughter Julie-Kate popped out of a huge cake to wish him happy birthday, and Peggy Ashcroft impersonated his old mentor Lilian Baylis: 'You did very well, Larry.' A year later came his last performance, a wheelchair-bound cameo in Derek Jarman's film *War Requiem.*

In March 1989 Laurence Olivier took a bad fall and shattered his hip. His sister Sybille died the next month, aged 87, and by 1 July he was not able to leave his bed. He was too weak to lift a glass; his nurse helped him, and once she spilled some juice onto his cheek. *My dear*, he said, *we are not doing fucking Hamlet.* Perhaps the nurse knew that, in the play within a play in *Hamlet,* poison is administered to the king through his ear.

It was one of the last things he said. Richard Olivier sent for his father's friend and agent Laurence Evans and Evans's wife Mary, and Joan flew back from filming in Los Angeles. A priest was called. Olivier would have liked that. He was not a religious man, but an actor knows that a priest lends gravitas to a deathbed. Besides, it would have reminded Olivier of his histrionic father, if he had been able to register the priest's arrival. But he could not. He had slipped into unconsciousness, from which he never emerged.

John Gielgud wrote to Joan Plowright, a letter which told her of his professional admiration for her husband, and hinted strongly at his personal ambivalence:

'. . . What a rich legacy he leaves behind; not only of his brilliant talents and extraordinary range of achievements – but the memory of his own vital courageous personality, his determination and power as performer, manager and director, the originality of his approach to every new and challenging venture, his physical bravery not only on the stage, but in the valiant way in which he faced his few failures and defeats, and above all his refusal to give up when he had become so ill.

'As you know we were never intimate friends over all these long years. He only spoke to me on one memorable day – I think it was just the time he had fallen in love with you. We talked at the Algonquin for about an hour and he told me of some of his tortured times with Vivien and a few other personal problems – a confidence that touched me very much. I was, I confess, always a bit afraid of him . . .

'I am sad not to have seen him these last years but I hesitated to intrude on the family life he had so richly deserved and I felt it might distress him to find me still lucky and well enough to go on working while he himself was so badly disabled . . .'

To someone else he said: 'I cannot help feeling sad, and somewhat ashamed too, that I did not strive to know him better, as our careers and ambitions spanned so many of the same years . . . To me he seemed personally rather secretive, and knowing my frivolous and often indiscreet nature, he never confided to me his fears or deepest thoughts . . . I shall always think of him as one of the most brilliant, gifted, indefatigable and controversial figures of our time . . .' Gielgud did not, notes his official biographer Sheridan Morley, use the word 'friend.'

Gielgud was irritated by the great, theatrical, over-the-top ceremony for Olivier at Westminster Abbey, and not entirely happy with the fate of Edmund Kean's sword, which he had given to Olivier. He had intended that it should be passed down from great actor to great actor, in the spirit that he had passed it to Olivier, not that it should be Olivier's in perpetuity.

The Olivier family gather at his memorial service at Westminster Abbey

Nonetheless, he agreed to read John Donne's sonnet *Death Be Not Proud* at the ceremony, and Alec Guinness was asked to make an eight-minute address. Guinness felt even more ambivalent than Gielgud, saying privately:

'Larry – I liked him and he was very nice to me but I knew how to survive him . . . He completely destroyed Redgrave. He tried to destroy Scofield, not deliberately but by animal cunning, instinctively. Also he could be very pretentious, do things quite unnecessarily, silly things to show off.' According to one of Guinness's biographers, Piers Paul Read, Guinness thought Olivier technically brilliant, but shallow. His address at Westminster Abbey was, of course, respectful, but even there he gave some insight into the man behind the actor.

Then there was a funeral at Olivier's local parish church where Anthony Hopkins read the final lines of *King Lear*, Olivier's last great acting triumph:

I have a journey, sir, shortly to go;
My master calls me, I must not say no.
The weight of this sad time we must obey;
Speak what we feel, not what we ought to say,
The oldest have born most: we that are young
Shall never see so much, or live so long.

Chronology

Year	Date	Life
1907		Laurence Kerr Olivier is born on 22 May in Dorking, Surrey.
1916	9	Plays Brutus in All Saint's production of *Julius Caesar*.
1922	15	Plays Katherine in a St Edward's School production of *The Taming of the Shrew*.
1924	17	Enrolls in Central School of Speech Training and Dramatic Art; professional London debut in *The Suliot Officer*.
1926	19	Joins the Birmingham Repertory.
1929	22	Film debut in *A Temporary Widow*.
1930	23	Marries Jill Esmond; *Private Lives* opens on Broadway.
1931	24	Signs first Hollywood contract with RKO.

Year	History	Culture
1907	Sun Yat-sen announces the programme of his Chinese Democratic Republic.	Conrad, *The Secret Agent*. S. Prokofiev, Undine. R. M. Rilke, *Neue Gedichte*.
1916	First Zeppelin raids on Paris; Battle of Verdun. Roger Casement executed. British first use tanks on Western Front.	F. Kafka, *The Judgement*. G. B. Shaw, *Pygmalion*.
1922	Mussolini's March on Rome. Atatürk declares Turkey a republic. Irish Free State proclaimed.	T. S. Eliot, *The Waste Land*. J. Joyce, *Ulysses*.
1924	Lenin dies; Stalin outmaneuvers Trotsky in race for succession.	E. M. Forster, *A Passage to India*. G. Gershwin, *Rhapsody in Blue*.
1926	Germany joins League of Nations. Hirohito becomes emperor of Japan.	M. Heidegger, *Being and Time*. Puccini, *Turandot*.
1929	Wall Street crash.	S. Dali, *The Great Masturbator*.
1930	M. Gandhi leads Salt March in India. Frank Whittle patents turbo-jet engine.	W. H. Auden, *Poems*. T. S. Eliot, *Ash Wednesday*.
1931	Japan occupies Manchuria. Building of Empire State Building completed in New York.	P. G. Wodehouse, *Big Money*. M. Yourcenar, *The New Eurydice*.

Year	Date	Life
1935	28	Alternates with John Gielgud playing Romeo in his London production of *Romeo and Juliet*; son Tarquin is born.
1936	29	With Ralph Richardson he directs his first play; and stars in his first Shakespearean film *As You Like It*.
1939	32	Returns to Hollywood to star as Heathcliff in *Wuthering Heights*, earning the first Oscar nomination.
1940	33	Lead role in Hitchcock's *Rebecca*; 31 August: divorces Jill Esmond and marries Vivien Leigh.
1941	34	Co-stars with Leigh in *That Hamilton Woman*.
1944	37	Produces, directs and stars in the film *Henry V*.
1947	40	Knighted.

Year	History	Culture
1935	In Germany, Nuremberg Laws enacted. Italy invades Abyssinia.	Marx Brothers, *A Night at the Opera*. G. Gershwin, *Porgy and Bess*.
1936	Edward VIII abdicates throne in Britain; George VI becomes king. Spanish Civil War (until 1939).	G. Orwell, *Keep the Aspidistra Flying*. O. Welles, 'voodoo' *Macbeth*. BBC public television founded.
1939	Germany invades Poland; Britain and France declare war on Germany.	Selznick, *Gone With the Wind*. Steinbeck, *Grapes of Wrath*.
1940	Germany occupies France, Belgium, the Netherlands, Norway and Denmark. In Britain, Winston Churchill becomes PM. Leon Trotsky assassinated in Mexico.	C. Chaplin, *The Great Dictator*. Disney, *Fantasia*. E. Hemingway, *For Whom the Bell Tolls*.
1941	Germany invades Soviet Union. Japan attacks Pearl Harbor: US enter Second World War.	B. Britten, *Paul Bunyan*. G. Orwell, *The Lion and the Unicorn*. O. Welles, *Citizen Kane*.
1944	Allies land in Normandy. Civil war in Greece.	J. L. Borges, *Fictions*. Eisenstein, *Ivan the Terrible*.
1947	India becomes independent. Chuck Yeager breaks the sound barrier.	T. Williams, *A Streetcar Named Desire*.

Year	Date	Life
1948	41	Wins Oscar for *Hamlet*.
1953	46	Movie singing debut in *The Beggars' Opera*.
1956	49	Plays Archie Rice in John Osborne's *The Entertainer*.
1957	50	Directing flop: with Marilyn Monroe in *The Prince and the Showgirl*.
1960	53	Divorce from Vivien Leigh; plays image-busting role as the ruthless, bisexual Crassus in *Spartacus*.
1961	54	Marries Joan Plowright (3 children: Julie-Kate, Tamsin and Richard).
1962	55	Named artistic director of the National Theatre.

Year	History	Culture
1948	Berlin Crisis. Gandhi is assassinated. State of Israel founded.	Greene, *The Heart of the Matter*. N. Mailer, *The Naked and the Dead*.
1953	Stalin dies. Korean War ends. Francis Crick and James Watson discover double helix (DNA).	F. Fellini, *I Vitelloni*. A. Miller, *The Crucible*. D. Thomas, *Under Milk Wood*.
1956	Suez Crisis. Revolts in Poland and Hungary.	L. Armstrong, *Mack the Knife*.
1957	EEC formed. USSR launches Sputnik.	B. Britten, *The Prince of the Pagodas*.
1960	Vietnam War begins (until 1975). OPEC formed. Oral contraceptives marketed.	B. Britten, *A Midsummer Night's Dream*. P. G.Wodehouse, *Jeeves in the Offing*.
1961	Berlin Wall erected. Bay of Pigs invasion. Yuri Gagarin is first man in space.	B. Britten, Cello Symphony. The Rolling Stones are formed. Rudolf Nureyev defects from USSR.
1962	Cuban missile crisis. Satellite television launched.	E. Albee, *Who's Afraid of Virginia Woolf?* D. Lean directs *Lawrence of Arabia*.

Year	Date	Life
1965	58	Plays fanatical Mahdi in *Khartoum*.
1970	63	Made a life peer.
1973	66	His performances in *Long Day's Journey Into Night* and *The Merchant of Venice* win him an Emmy nomination in two categories.
1974	67	Last stage appearance.
1979	72	Receives honorary Oscar for his life's work.
1980	73	*The Jazz Singer*.

Year	History	Culture
1965	Military coup in Indonesia.	N. Simon, *The Odd Couple*.
1970	G. Nasser and C. de Gaulle die. S. Allende elected President of Chile.	I. Murdoch, *A Fairly Honorable Defeat*. M. Spark, *The Driver's Seat*.
1973	Yom Kippur War. Denmark, Ireland and Britain enter EC. US withdraws from Vietnam War. OPEC oil crisis.	Pink Floyd, *The Dark Side of the Moon*. Larkin, *High Windows*. Truffaut, *Day for Night*.
1974	Watergate scandal. Cyprus invaded by Turkey. Haile Selassie deposed in Ethiopia.	Solzhenitsyn is expelled from the Soviet Union. Polanski (producer) *Chinatown*.
1979	Shah of Iran is forced into exile. Idi Amin overthrown. Camp David Accords. Z. Bhutto hanged. M. Thatcher elected British PM.	P. Shaffer, *Amadeus*. Herbert Marcuse, Ger.-born Amer. philosopher and guru of sixties revolutionary movements, dies (b. 1898).
1980	A. Sakharov sent into exile in Gorki. US diplomats held hostage in Iran. Zimbabwe becomes independent. Lech Walesa becomes head of Polish trade union Solidarity.	I. Murdoch, *Nuns and Soldiers*. Le Carré, *Smiley's People*. J. Lennon is shot. Hitchcock, Eng.-born Amer. film director, dies. Kokoschka, Austrian painter, dies.

Year	Date	Life
1981	74	Stars in *Inchon*.
1982	75	Publishes autobiography *Confessions of an Actor*.
1983	76	Shines in television production of *Mister Halpern and Mister Johnson*.
1984	77	*King Lear* on television.
1986	79	Publishes *On Acting*.
1988	81	Last appearance in the film *War Requiem*.
1989	82	Dies on 11 July in Steyning, West Sussex; interred at Westminster Abbey, London.

Year	History	Culture
1981	Greece joins the EC. R. Reagan becomes US President.	E. Canetti wins Nobel Prize for Literature. S. Rushdie, *Midnight's Children* wins Booker Prize.
1982	Argentine forces invade Falkland Islands.	Elizabeth Taylor makes her London theatrical debut.
1983	START talks between USSR and US about arms reduction.	Ralph Richardson dies. *M*A*S*H* ends after 251 episodes.
1984	US peacekeeping forces withdrawn from Lebanon.	Ted Hughes becomes new Poet Laureate.
1986	Portugal and Spain enter EC. Swedish PM Palme shot.	News Int. moves the *Times* out of London's Fleet St despite strike.
1988	Palestinian Intifada begins.	P. Brooks stages *Mahabharatha* in Glasgow.
1989	Soviet troops leave Afghanistan. Czech playwright V. Havel becomes president.	Muslim protests against S. Rushdie's novel *Satanic Verses*. Archaeologists uncover Shakespeare's Globe Theatre.

Further Reading

Books by Laurence Olivier

Olivier, Laurence, *Confessions of an Actor* (London, 1982).
Olivier, Laurence, *On Acting* (London, 1986).

Biographies of Laurence Olivier

Bragg, Melvyn, *Laurence Olivier* (London, 1989).
Lewis, Roger, *The Real Life of Laurence Olivier* (London, 1996).
Spoto, Donald, *Laurence Olivier* (New York, 1992).

Other biographies

Croall, Jonathan, *Gielgud, A Theatrical Life* (London, 2000).
Morley, Sheridan, *The Authorised Biography of John Gielgud* (London, 2001).
O'Connor, Garry, *Alec Guinness, Master of Disguise* (London, 1994).
O'Connor, Garry, *Ralph Richardson, An Actor's Life* (London, 1999).
Osborne, John, *Looking Back* (London, 1999).
Plowright, Joan, *Memoirs – And That's Not All* (London, 2001).
Read, Piers Paul, *The Authorised Biography of Alec Guinness* (London, 2003).
Redgrave, Corin, *Michael Redgrave – My Father* (London, 1995).

Other books

Steinberg, Micheline, *Flashback – 100 Years of Stratford-upon-Avon and the Royal Shakespeare Company* (Stratford-upon-Avon, 1985).

Trussler, Simon, *The Cambridge Illustrated History of British Theatre* (Cambridge, 1994).

Picture Sources

The author and publishers wish to express their thanks to the following sources of illustrative material and/or permission to reproduce it. They will make proper acknowledgements in future editions in the event that any omissions have occurred.

Album akg Images: p. 50; Getty Images: pp. 7, 10, 12, 18, 23, 26, 28, 39, 52, 56, 63, 66, 71, 73, 80, 91, 103, 125, 127, 140; Topham Picturepoint: pp. 31, 36, 42, 55, 59, 73, 77, 94, 96, 118, 134.

Index